THE BLUE BERETS

The
Blue Berets

MICHAEL HARBOTTLE

STACKPOLE BOOKS

First published in the United States of America 1972 by

STACKPOLE BOOKS
Cameron & Kelker Streets,
Harrisburg, Pa. 17105

Copyright © 1971 *Michael Harbottle*

Printed in Great Britain at
the Pitman Press, Bath

To Eirwen

CONTENTS

ILLUSTRATIONS

MAPS

AUTHOR'S NOTE

This is a guide book to the more prominent of the peacekeeping efforts that the United Nations have mounted over the last twenty-five years. It does no more than briefly describe the causes and effects of each conflict, the conduct of the operations themselves and adds a few basic statistics that can help the reader to count the cost in terms of peace or war. It is neither meant to be a history book nor an educational manual, but it does seek to be regarded through its comprehensive bibliography as a book of reference for those who are interested in the subject of international relations, the objectives of international organizations, and the detailed study of conflict management.

The book does not attempt, for obvious reasons of space, to record and analyse the lessons to be learnt from each particular operation or mission, but in the concluding chapter a brief evaluation is made of the machinery of peacekeeping and of its effective working to date.

But essentially this is an attempt to set forth in a straightforward and easily digestible form the facts about this greatest and most enduring practical peace effort of all times—a peace effort which should have pride of place in history books; a story of considerable achievement that is not generally known nor appreciated by the vast majority of people in this country, or in the world. It is a record of success rather than failure, for it is in degrees of success that the operations of the UN peace forces and missions can be measured. If it does nothing else, it is hoped that the book will make people aware of the immense contribution that certain individuals and countries have made to the maintenance of international peace during the past quarter century.

CHAPTER 1

Introduction — The Rules of the Game

Before embarking upon a study of UN peacekeeping, some of the governing factors need to be understood so that any later evaluation is set against a correct backcloth and in proper perspective. For, as in everything else, the rules dictate the manner of the play.

To begin with, it is the Security Council that has the authority under the United Nations Charter to 'take such action by air, sea or land forces as may be necessary to maintain or restore international peace'. Over the years, this authority to use enforcement action has been tempered to that of peaceable intervention, in order to meet political expedience. With the exception of the Korean war,* all UN peacekeeping operations and missions have been at the request of, or with the consent of, one or all of the parties concerned—the 'host' country or countries. In any event the power of the veto, which can be exercised by any of the permanent members of the Security Council, Britain, France, Nationalist China, USA and USSR, can render powerless the peace initiatives of the Council and can be effectively used to block the adoption of any resolution before it. It is difficult to foresee any circumstance in which there would be unanimity among the four big powers in respect of international

* See Chapter 7.

enforcement action. There are, however, ways in which a deadlock in the Security Council can be overcome through action by the General Assembly, but in the process the authority becomes weaker.* Even the practice of peaceable intervention is invariably challenged by France and Russia as having no legal status under the Charter, though this has not prevented them from supporting resolutions approving it in the past.

This rigid political control over the UN's military operations has not helped to simplify or make more efficient the peacekeeping machinery. The Military Staff Committee, established under Article 47 of the Charter to advise and assist the Security Council, has for years been a committee in name only. There is no operative military staff at UN Headquarters available for operational and logistic planning. For ten years, from 1958 to 1969, the Secretary-General had a Military Adviser, General Indar Jit Rikhye of India, but when he left UN service the post lapsed. All UN military peacekeeping operations are mounted by the UN Secretariat in conjunction with the contributing countries which agree to provide contingents. There are no months of planning, no opportunities for reconnaissance; there is no stand-by professional military force or built-in administrative/logistic support. When the whistle blows everything has to be put together from whatever resources might become available and assembled, in the fashion of a meccano set, to match the requirements of the moment. The call for help to the United Nations often comes suddenly, insistently and without temporizing from the government or governments concerned. Until the decision has been taken in the Security Council authorizing the Secretary-General to go ahead with establishing the Force or Mission, only the most tentative soundings can be made towards raising the kind of force that will be required. Any military operation requires careful planning, sound organization and an administrative backing that will ensure that the force

* See Chapter 2.

deployed is well-found from the start. All this is well-known to the student of military history and needs no further comment; he also knows that on many occasions insufficient and slipshod preparations have turned success into failure. The *ad hoc* has never been a successful counter to the deliberate. But the lack of any pre-planning and preparation, and the fact that there is no ready-made UN army standing by, makes the *ad hoc* unavoidable, and until a more realistic attitude is adopted within the United Nations there is little likelihood of the existing brand of instant peacekeeping being replaced by anything more deliberate.

Certain countries, in particular the Nordic countries, retain specific units which have been earmarked for service with the UN. Because of the relative smallness of their armed forces, they rely on volunteer reservists to man these units. This is why so many of the soldiers serving in peacekeeping operations are volunteers. On the other hand contingents found by Canada, India and Pakistan contain 100 per cent Regulars (as Britain's is in Cyprus). The Irish make up their successive contingents with volunteers from throughout their regular army, with the result that man for man the Irish soldier is probably the most experienced UN soldier there is—some having served five or six times on peacekeeping operations. Over the years, these contributing countries have taken part in most of the operations that the UN has mounted, but they are by no means the only ones. One of the rules of the game is that the host country has a right to say what nationalities it is prepared to accept on its territory. This can pose great difficulties for those in the UN responsible for finding contingents—a total of 35 contingents were needed for the Congo. Also, at the time of Suez it was mutually agreed by the permanent members of the Security Council that it would be undesirable for them to provide contingents for UN peacekeeping—a decision that has been modified since by Britain's participation in the UN Force in Cyprus.

However, one must not lose sight of the fact that under currently accepted principles the deployment of any UN peace-keeping operation or military observer mission is dependent upon it being requested or accepted; without that request or consent there could be no peacekeeping—a sobering thought when international peace is in the balance, but also a rational approach when one considers the inherent dangers in a third-party enforcement action. One does not have to look far for examples of the latter; they are reported daily in the newspapers. Britain's military enforcement actions in Palestine, Cyprus and Aden were, to say the least, inconclusive.

The 'use of force', however minimal, is a prerequisite of the enforcement action, whether it is in Czechoslovakia, Vietnam or Northern Ireland. It plays no part in the peacekeeping operations of the United Nations—the peaceable intervention. Here the UN soldier only uses the weapon he is armed with for self-defence purposes in the event of his being attacked. In all other instances he will use the 'weapons' of negotiation, reason and quiet diplomacy to settle arguments and defuse crisis situations, not his self-loading rifle.

It might be hard to believe that without the authority of a rifle a soldier can achieve very much in the way of peacekeeping, when the contestants are so obviously anxious to get at each other's throats; but he can and he does. The rifle he carries provides him with his means of self-protection, not a passport for violence. One must remember that the kind of operations in which the British Army has been involved over the last two decades have been 'operations in aid of the civil power' where minimum force can mean anything from a single round over the heads of a crowd to a full-scale company attack against insurgents' positions. Although this is commonly referred to as peacekeeping, it is not peacekeeping in the true sense. Peacekeeping is an impartial act and impartiality in this context means non-alignment with either side in a dispute, ideally to the extent of total detachment from the controversial issues at stake. It is important to understand the distinction when reading this book.

But whatever one says, these restrictions on the use of force are a severe test of the UN soldier's ingenuity and an understandable limitation to the extent of his authoritative powers. The essential qualities of training, discipline and courage are as important to his make-up as to any other soldier of any army; but more than this he requires to have the intuitive touch of a diplomat, the patience of a Job and the imperturbability of a Buddha, whether he be a private soldier or the Force Commander himself, for negotiations takes place at all levels and it is often the success of the most junior rank on the spot that prevents the escalation of a local incident into a larger conflict. It is a role that depends on words rather than deeds for its success and it is in this context that this book should be read.

CHAPTER 2

Egypt 1956-1967

I

The story of the United Nations Emergency Force
(UNEF) could well be accorded the title 'Alpha and Omega',
the Beginning and the End; for it is its beginning and end which
have been remembered and chronicled, while its middle has gone
virtually unrecorded and unnoticed. This, of course, is the
measure of UNEF's achievement, in that it maintained a stable
peaceful situation in the Gaza Strip and along the length of the
Egypt–Israel International Frontier Line for more than ten
years and thereby contributed in no small degree to the avoid-
ance of war in the Middle East during that period. Maybe it did
not solve anything, but then peace forces are not designed to
find solutions to political disputes, nor to solve the problems
that arise from the racial, social, economic and ethnic differences
existing between peoples who geographically are neighbours but
whose respective sympathies and understanding are sadly at
variance. UNEF's *raison d'être* was to achieve a military disengagement and thereafter to re-establish stability and order in
the situation whereby the opportunities for a peaceful settlement of the political dispute could be better developed. The
extent to which it succeeded can best be described by quoting
the Secretary-General's final report on the UNEF operation,
made in July 1967.*

'The recent tragic events in the Near East that followed
UNEF's withdrawal . . . do not obscure, but rather under-
score, the achievements of UNEF as a unique peacekeeping
venture. When, in March 1957, UNEF reached the International Frontier in Sinai and the Armistice Demarcation Line

* A/6672 of 12 July, 1967.

in the Gaza Strip . . . it was deployed along what had been only four months before one of the most troubled borders anywhere in the world. With UNEF's deployment there, that line became and remained almost completely quiet. The terrorizing raids of the "fedayeen"* across that line into Israel became a thing of the past. Infiltration across the line from either side was almost ended. Fields near the line on both sides, which for long had been left uncultivated because it was near suicide to come into view in the open fields, were now being worked right up to the line itself and on both sides of it.† Costly irrigation systems were extensively installed. Heavy investments in new citrus groves and in other cash crops were made. A new prosperity came to the area in UNEF's decade . . . because of UNEF's effective buffer role, there was security as there was no longer a military confrontation between the armed forces of Israel and the United Arab Republic. . . . In consequence, there was throughout Gaza and Sinai an unaccustomed quiet for more than ten years. . . .' When eventually war did come it was not as a result of the failure of UNEF to fulfil its responsibilities.

Equally significant were UNEF's relationships with the local population and local authorities. These continued to be excellent until the last few days of its presence. Based on tact and understanding, the attitude of the Force inspired confidence and trust in the people for whom they were keeping the peace. Good relations were of crucial importance to the continuance of the UN presence, for without them it would have been impossible for the peacekeeping operation to have maintained itself or to have functioned for very long. Anyone who has served in a UN peace mission will know how important it is to the conduct of the operation for that friendly understanding to exist. In Egypt, had it not been maintained, the request for UNEF's withdrawal could have come much earlier than it did.

* Palestinian commandos.
† There is an analogy to this in the Cyprus operation.

It is therefore its beginning and end that this account of UNEF concentrates upon—its establishment and disestablishment. The latter has been the subject of much controversy and misrepresentation, some incredibly naive and irresponsible, but it is certainly neither fair nor objective to adjudge UNEF a failure, as many people have, on the grounds that it was withdrawn when it was most needed. The political and procedural arguments will no doubt continue for a long time, but the performance of UNEF and its achievements in its peacekeeping role are not subject to argument. Placed in its proper perspective it is a story of success, not of failure.

2

The Middle East since the end of the Second World War has seldom been off the front pages of the world press. For the last twenty-two years there has been a United Nations peace-keeping presence in the area. The first of these was the Truce Supervision organization (UNTSO). It is (for it still continues) an observer group charged with supervising the observance by both sides of the armistice agreements drawn up after the Arab/ Israel war of 1948 and with reporting any violation of the armistice demarcation lines and demilitarized zones established by those agreements.

UNEF was a totally separate operation, though it did lean heavily at first on the existing organization of UNTSO and later was bound up with it in the general problem of the Middle East.

During 1956 an already volatile and explosive situation in the Middle East worsened. The fedayeen had stepped up their attacks into Israel and Israeli retaliation had become more severe. Egypt had earlier closed the Suez Canal to Israeli shipping and had blockaded the Gulf of Aqaba, Israel's only access to the Red Sea. This ever-tightening stranglehold on her economic outlets and the increasing irritation of the fedayen raids

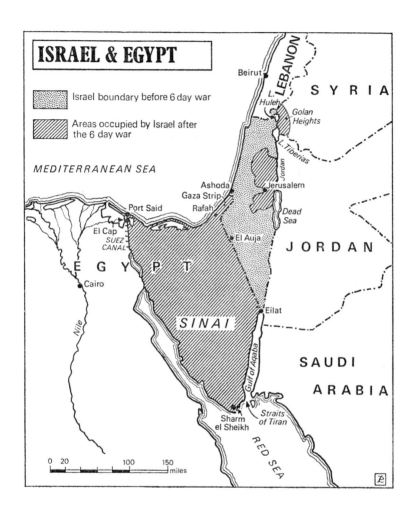

had a cumulative effect on Israel and on 29 October her forces advanced into Egypt. The Egyptian army in the Sinai were no match for her highly trained and mobile columns and in a very short time the Israelis had reached the Gulf of Aqaba and had captured Sharm el Shekh at its entrance, where the Egyptians had installed naval guns to prevent Israeli ships from passing through the Straits of Tiran into the Red Sea.

At that time President Nasser was also in trouble with Britain and France over his seizure of the Suez Canal. In July 1956, he had arbitrarily nationalized the Canal. This national take-over of an international waterway represented a direct threat to Europe's oil supplies, particularly those of England and France. Freedom of use of the Canal was no longer guaranteed since it would be in the power of Egypt to close it at any time. Attempts to come to a satisfactory agreement on safeguards failed to make progress, so the matter was referred to the United Nations where on 12 October the Secretary-General published a six-point draft of an agreement, which the Security Council endorsed the next day. However, Britain and France were bent on more positive action. During September the former reinforced Cyprus with a number of infantry regiments and in October French paratroops joined those of Britain already on the island.

The day following Israel's attack on Egypt, Britain and France called on both countries to stop fighting and to withdraw to a distance of ten miles from the Canal (since Israel's advance had not yet reached that point, the Anglo-French ultimatum did nothing to halt her advance). Not surprisingly Egypt totally rejected the ultimatum, refusing to stop fighting in defence of her country. On the ground that they were acting to protect the Suez Canal and to halt the fighting, Britain and France intervened by mounting a joint air offensive against Egypt's airfields on 31 October. The aerial bombing and strafing from bases in Cyprus lasted five days, but far from protecting the Canal it caused Nasser to sink blockships across it. On 5 November the ground phase of the operation began with combined British and French airborne and seaborne assaults from bases in Cyprus and Malta. In all about 20,000 troops were put ashore. The ensuing fighting lasted less than 24 hours before Britain and France agreed to abide by a United Nations call for a ceasefire and to the establishment of an international peace force under the UN flag. So the fighting came to an end before any of the Anglo-French objectives had been achieved. On the other hand, Israel had gained all hers and was happy to accept the ceasefire, though she was to stand firm on the ground she had gained long after the United Nations had demanded her withdrawal.

It is not the intention here to embark on an appraisal of the Anglo-French action, nor to comment on the controversial nature of the decisions taken. Other works have already done this most comprehensively. It is with what followed that we are concerned here.

3

On 3 November the General Assembly adopted a resolution, sponsored by Canada, calling for the setting up of 'an emergency international force to secure and supervise a cease-fire' in Egypt. On the same day, a second resolution was adopted authorizing the Secretary-General 'to arrange with the parties concerned for the implementation of the cease-fire and the halting of the movement of military forces and arms into the area . . .'. On 5 November a further General Assembly resolution authorized the raising of a United Nations Command for the purposes set out in the Canadian resolution, and the Chief of Staff of UNTSO, Major-General E. L. M. Burns (fittingly enough himself a Canadian) was appointed its first commander. There was no delay on the part of any of the combatants to accept the cease-fire call or to recognize the establishment of the Emergency Force; though the Prime Minister of Israel, Ben Gurion, did declare in a broadcast on the 7 November that 'Israel would not accept foreign troops upon her soil'.

It may be wondered why it was the General Assembly which took action on this occasion and not the Security Council, the executive body empowered by the United Nations Charter to take action to restore or maintain international peace. The short answer is that two of the permanent member states of the Council, Britain and France, had vetoed an earlier resolution before it calling on the parties concerned to 'refrain from the use of force . . . in the area . . . and to assist the United Nations in ensuring the integrity of the armistic agreement between Egypt and Israel'. Since a veto by a permanent member automatically bars the adoption of a resolution, it was unlikely that the Council would have been able to take action in accordance with its powers. The General Assembly, at the time of the Korean war in 1950, had foreseen the possibility of such an impasse and had passed a resolution that 'if the Security Council, because of lack of unanimity of the permanent members, fails to exercise its primary responsibility for the maintenance of peace and security in any case where there appears to be a threat to the peace, breach of the peace, or act of aggression, the General Assembly shall consider the matter immediately with a view to making appropriate recommendations to Members for collective measures . . . to maintain or restore international peace and security'.* There were, however, limitations to how far the General Assembly could go. It could establish a force but it could not impose it upon the territory of any state without the consent of the government of that state—a limitation to which the Security Council is not subject.† Since Israel had already made it clear that she would not have foreign troops on her soil, Egypt's agreement to the stationing of the Force on her territory, therefore, was a vital pre-requisite to UNEF's establishment. By the same token the composition of a Force needs to be acceptable to the 'host' country. Though the prerogative of decision lies

* Called the 'Uniting for Peace' Resolution.
† Chapter VII of the Charter empowers the Security Council to use enforcement measures where considered necessary to maintain international peace.

with the United Nations, it is clearly in the interests of the peacekeeping operation that those national contingents making up the Force should be acceptable to the government on whose territory they are to be stationed. The use of the 'blackball' by the 'host' country should not of course be arbitrary, but on the other hand, as host it could not be expected to accept a contingent from a country which was out of sympathy with its policies.

These two criteria delayed the arrival of UNEF at Port Said until 15 November and necessitated Dag Hammarskjöld flying to Cairo to negotiate the terms under which the Force would operate. In the belief that a satisfactory agreement would be reached, the Secretary-General had already persuaded the Italian government to allow the UN to use Capodichino, near Naples, as a staging area, and the build-up of the Force was proceeding whilst Hammarskjöld and Nasser were conferring in Cairo. UNEF's initial strength was to be 3,500, but later when the Force moved up into Sinai, General Burns estimated that his requirement would be for two combat brigades, plus logistic support—6,000 men.

A total of twenty-four member states offered contingents from whom the Secretary-General selected ten: Brazil, Canada, Colombia, Denmark, Finland, India, Indonesia, Norway, Sweden and Yugoslavia. At first Nasser declined Canada's offer, not on political grounds but rather because her soldiers might easily be mistaken by Egyptians for British soldiers*; however, a compromise was reached whereby the Canadians were to be kept in reserve, though later they provided the bulk of the logistic support, an armoured car squadron and a signals troop. General Burns himself was not immune from this 'base calumny', for it was pointed out to him soon after his arrival in Port Said that he looked every inch a British officer in his

---

* A battalion of the Canadian Black Watch had been chosen and it was ready and waiting at Capodichino.

battledress and that he should do something fairly quick about it. His reaction was to signal to a military tailor in London for a Royal Air Force service dress hat, specifically stating 'but it is to be without the RAF badge'; from then on his identity went unchallenged. Burns brought with him a number of his own officers from UNTSO who provided the staff for his head-quarters until the arrival of others belonging to those countries providing contingents. To assist the Secretary-General in his collection and organization of the Force a small planning staff, composed of military representatives from those countries con-tributing troops to UNEF, was set up in New York to advise him on all military matters concerned with the operation in its early stages. This temporary advisory body made an invaluable contribution, but even its efforts did not prevent some of the chaos and disorganization that is attendant upon instant *ad hoc* military operations. For example, six of the battalions, on arrival in Egypt, found themselves marooned in the sand dunes with only ten days' rations, without transport or medical supplies, and lacking a staff.

The view that there should be a permanent contingency plan-ning staff at United Nations Headquarters is held by a number of former UN field commanders and senior staff officers from Egypt, the Congo and Cyprus. So far the idea has not found favour within the United Nations, largely for political reasons. The Organization is a civilian body not a military one and it is a political not a military decision that initiates a peacekeeping operation. However, very tangible reasons exist for having an advisory planning staff at UN Headquarters, and these will be discussed later. For UNEF, the experiment of having even a temporary body to advise the Secretary-General paid substantial dividends. Dag Hammarskjöld's was an incredible achievement in getting the Force into position and operational in such a short time; incredible when you consider that the whole responsibility for setting it up, negotiating its terms of action, deciding on

its composition and drawing up its regulations and instructions
had been laid firmly upon his shoulders by the General Assembly, along with the other responsibilities it had placed on him
concerning the cease-fire, the withdrawal of Israel to behind the
Armistice Line, the withdrawal of the British and French forces
and, last but not least, the financing of the operation to come.

4

The first contingents of UNEF began arriving in the Canal
Zone on 15 November; they were those from Colombia, Denmark, Norway. Shortly afterwards came the Canadians, Finns,
Indians, Swedes and Yugoslavs. Their first task was to interpose
themselves between the British and French forces on the one
side and the Egyptians on the other. To achieve this, they occupied a small buffer zone among the dunes between El Cap and
Port Said. This period did not last long, for it had been the
undertaking of the British and French Governments to withdraw their forces as soon as UNEF had taken up position and
was in control. Even so, the withdrawal was not completed until
22 December, a delay which prompted more than one resolution
of disapproval by the General Assembly.

UNEF's interposition at this moment of tension helped in
restoring and maintaining calm among the civilian population.
Although the welcome given to the first arrivals was boisterous,
it was tinged with relief. But calm did not come overnight—
there were still the periodic outbreaks of shooting, despite the
ceasefire. Besides patrolling and guarding the buffer zone, the
UN assisted the local authorities in keeping order; they supervised the exchange of prisoners; they undertook the guarding
of vital installations and of the salvage ships clearing the Canal.
Finally they cordoned-off the embarkation points being used by
the British and French for the withdrawal of their troops. All

this was done quietly and with good faith and helped to defuse the situation.

On the day that the last Anglo-French troops left Egyptian soil, Israel began to withdraw her troops from the east bank of the Canal back behind the Armistice Line, but she refused to relinquish Sharm el Sheikh and the Gulf of Aqaba until there were guarantees that these would be taken over by the United Nations Force so that Egypt would be prevented from re-imposing her blockade of the Gulf. It was to be some months before Israel finally withdrew from this area.

Nasser, in agreeing to the presence of UNEF in the Port Said area, had advised the Secretary-General that once the withdrawal of the Anglo-French and Israeli forces from the Canal zone had been completed, he did not wish UNEF to remain there but to move into Sinai to ensure the total withdrawal of the Israelis to behind the original Armistice Line. This require-ment had not been stipulated in the resolutions of the General Assembly which had envisaged the Force solely supervising the cease-fire and withdrawal of the foreign troops from the Canal zone. There was a division of opinion regarding UNEF's further role, but eventually the Assembly approved the continu-ation of the operation and the deployment of UNEF along the Egyptian-Israeli Armistice Demarcation Line, 'after the full withdrawal by Israel from Sharm el Shekh and Gaza areas', to assist in maintaining peace.

This was the beginning of Phase 2 of the UNEF operation. With the departure of the Anglo-French force there was no further cause for UNEF to remain in the Port Said area. The Israelis had begun their slow withdrawal back from the Canal and step by step as they moved back, so step by step did UNEF move forward into Sinai taking over areas as they were evacu-ated by the Israelis; remaining as a buffer between the two armies to prevent a recurrence in the fighting. As each stage progressed, minefields were cleared, the installations were repaired and got working again; and, as in Phase 1, UNEF arranged and supervised the exchange of prisoners between the two sides. The Brazilians had by now joined the Force, which had reached its planned strength of 6,000.

By 22 January, 1957, the bulk of the Israeli army was back behind the demarcation line, but it was to be another two months before Israel withdrew from Sharm el Shekh and the Gaza Strip. The particular significance that the former had for Israel has already been explained. It was her sole outlet to the Red Sea and she was determined not to see it blocked again. She wanted the UN to establish a presence there before she withdrew a single soldier. In a broadcast on the day after Israel had completed her withdrawal in Sinai, Prime Minister Ben Gurion declared that there could be no withdrawal from the Gulf of Aqaba until firm guarantees had been provided for the freedom of navigation through it of all Israeli ships, as well as those of the rest of the world. The uncertainty of tenure of UNEF did not provide such a guarantee so far as Israel was concerned and therefore more binding and lasting guarantees were necessary before she could contemplate withdrawing her forces from the Gulf.

The problem relating to the Gaza Strip was slightly different but no less pertinent to her security requirements so far as Israel was concerned. It was from this area of 210 square miles that the fedayeen had mounted the majority of their attacks against Israel, which had in part contributed to the war just ended. There was no reason to suppose that the fedayeen would not renew their attacks once they had regained their base of operations. Israel's demands for the neutralization of this threat to her security were therefore as insistent and obdurate as those concerning the Gulf of Aqaba.

It took a long time to persuade the Israeli Government to modify its position. No assurances came from Egypt that she would not revert to her former policy once she regained control of the Gulf. Israel's compliance with the General Assembly's resolution calling for her complete withdrawal was therefore dependent upon the UN's capacity to ensure that her fears were not realized. UNEF was no occupying army. Its responsibility was to see that the disengagement was achieved and to keep it that way until such a time as a lasting and peaceful settlement was reached between Arab and Jew. Eventually Israel had to be satisfied with this and accede to the UN's urgings. After much diplomatic inter-play, she agreed to withdraw from both Gaza and Sharm el Shekh, and these withdrawals took place on 6 and 8 March respectively. Before evacuating Sharm el Shekh the Israeli army destroyed all the Egyptian pillboxes and gun emplacements, putting out of action the 6-inch naval guns that had hitherto controlled the shipping lanes through the Straits of Tiran—the entrance to the Gulf. As the Israelis withdrew, UNEF moved in her troops; the Canadians, Danes, Indians, Norwegians and Swedes into the Gaza Strip and the Finns into Sharm el Shekh.

5

Phase 2 was over. Phase 3 was beginning and was to last ten more years. It got off to a slightly turbulent start when General Burns appointed a Danish officer, Colonel Carl Ingholm, as military governor of Gaza. Rioting broke out throughout the town at the news, and there were demands for the return of the Egyptian administration; the honeymoon, at least temporarily, was over. For a while UNEF became the aggressors—'an occupation force all too ready to impose its own rules on the people of Gaza'. Its vehicles were stoned and an attempt was made to break into the UN headquarters, but this attack was repulsed when Danish and Norwegian troops fired over the heads of the rioters. It was unfortunate that in this shooting one Arab was killed, for it only helped to increase tension. Nor was the Egyptian Government tardy in its reaction. It accused UNEF of acting contrary to the conditions governing its presence in Egypt which had been agreed between the Government and the UN. Hurriedly Cairo appointed a Colonel Latif as governor of Gaza. Latif's immediate action on arrival was to impose a curfew which remained in force until tempers had subsided and calm had returned. From then on there was rarely trouble between the inhabitants and UNEF. The co-existence of the military staffs of Egypt and UNEF appears to have run a smooth course right up to the end. Dr Bunche, on a visit to Cairo at the end of March for discussions with President Nasser, made it clear in a press statement that the UN would give full co-operation to the new Egyptian administration in Gaza—a statement which in no way pleased the Israelis. There had been renewed fedayeen terrorism during February and March and it was no surprise that this reassumption of control over the town by the Egyptians aroused much indignation and suspicion in Israel. She had insisted that one condition of her withdrawal was that Egypt would not be allowed to regain control in the Gaza Strip and in the words of Ben Gurion, ' . . . Israel felt justified in using military force if there was a return to the *status quo ante* in the Gaza area . . . '. But this temporary threat to UNEF's mission was dissipated by careful and tactful handling and UNEF proceeded to its task of re-establishing a peaceful zone astride the armistice demarcation line.

UNEF'S inherent weakness, however, and one which was to play a significant part in the final days of its existence, was that from the start the Israeli Government adamantly refused to allow any part of the Force to be stationed on her side of the demarcation line. Had she at any time acceded to the General Assembly's urgings that she should do so, it might have avoided the outbreak of hostilities in 1967—only might have, because if two opponents are determined to have a battle there is little or nothing that a third party can do to stop it. Israel's claim was that the provocation that brought about the war of 1956 was all on the side of Egypt, by her denial of freedom of passage for Israel's ships through the Gulf of Aqaba and the ever-increasing intensity of fedayeen raids across Israel's southern frontier. Were she to give her consent to the stationing of UN troops on her territory it would, in her opinion, be tantamount to an admission of guilt for what had happened; and this was an admission Israel was not prepared to make. For more than ten years she ignored any suggestion that she should reconsider her decision and when, at Egypt's insistence, UNEF was required to leave Egyptian soil and a final attempt was made to persuade Israel to allow the Force to move across to her side of the line, she replied with a blank refusal. No doubt by then action had overtaken events, and decision had passed the point of no return. Another round in the Arab-Jew conflict was due and there was no denying it.

The antecedents of this next round—the Six Day War of June, 1967—lay in the continuing military and political confrontation existing between Israel and her Arab neighbours—the two explosive ingredients of the Arab-Israel conflict. These, as formerly, were the abrasive elements which triggered-off the war of 1967. Too many place the blame on the UN's 'impetuous' withdrawal whereby the chock holding in place the floodgates of war was removed. Incredibly, one former British politician blames Secretary-General U Thant for starting the war!* In demanding the removal of the UN presence, the Egyptian Government was simply clearing the decks for action. There had been no deterioration in the situation in the Gaza Strip, nor along Egypt's frontier with Israel, but for some months there had been a worsening in Israeli-Syrian relations. Syria considered herself threatened by attack from Israel and looked to

* Lord George Brown.

Nasser for help. Nasser, wishing to show solidarity with his ally, sought to clear aside any obstacle that might prevent his going to Syria's aid if she were attacked.

The controversy that has surrounded the whole circumstance of the withdrawal should not be allowed to detract from the achievement of UNEF. Unfortunately, the success of UNEF's peacekeeping efforts had induced a political euphoria amounting to a marked lack of urgency in the quest of a settlement on the part of those most closely concerned; and a lack of a positive initiative or constructive mediation effort by the United Nations. The lost opportunity seems difficult to understand; but it needs to be remembered that the Middle East over this period was anything but peaceful. The continuing operation of the Truce Supervision Organization (UNTSO) and the Observer missions to the Lebanon (UNOGIL) and Yemen (UNYOM)† underline the effort that was being put into the Middle East by the United Nations; but without a comparable effort to achieve a political settlement, their efforts were being squandered. One clear lesson that came from the UNEF operation (and one which has been demonstrated since in Cyprus) is that peacekeeping alone is not enough; it and peacemaking (mediation) must be an integrated effort. Alone, peacekeeping can only achieve a *status quo*—a fossilization of the situation—and this in the end helps no one and solves nothing.

6

At 8 p.m. on 16 May, 1967, General Rikhye, UNEF Commander, was handed a message from General Fawzy, Chief of Staff of the United Arab Republic Armed Forces, requesting him to withdraw all UN troops from their OPs along the Egyptian

† See p. 110

border. He was also informed by Brigadier Mokhtar, who had brought the message, that he must order the immediate with-drawal of the UN troops from Sharm el Sheikh, to be completed that same night, as the Egyptian army needed to occupy it. General Rikhye naturally refused to act on these instructions, pointing out that he could not in any way relinquish or abandon his position except on the instructions of the Secretary-General. Until such orders were received he was in duty bound to con-tinue to operate as hitherto, nor would he be dissuaded from this position, despite the warning from Brigadier Mokhtar that it might mean fighting between UN and United Arab Republic troops. Even the Brigadier's plea that UN troops should be con-fined to their camps made no impression on General Rikhye, who rightly insisted that any changes in UNEF's present deploy-ment and movements could only be ordered by the Secretary-General. Rikhye then cabled the contents of General Fawzy's message and the gist of Brigadier Mokhtar's additional require-ments to the Secretary-General, whose reply was for UNEF to stand firm and relinquish nothing. There followed intensive diplomatic activity in New York between the Secretary-General and the UN's Permanent Representative of the United Arab Republic, the outcome of which was a confirmation that it was Egypt's desire that the UN Force should be withdrawn and as speedily as possible. U Thant, deeply concerned at the likely repercussions following UNEF's withdrawal, attempted a per-sonal appeal to Nasser but was brusquely told by Egypt's Foreign Minister that such an appeal would be unwise and un-availing as President Nasser would not entertain any question of UNEF remaining. An offer by U Thant to go to Cairo was, however, accepted. From the time he received Rikhye's signal the Secretary-General remained in close consultation with the UN Advisory Committee (a group of member states selected by the General Assembly in 1956 to assist the Secretary-General in the fulfilment of his responsibilities in respect of the

Count Folke Bernadotte.

2. General Burns (left), Commander of UNEF, in Port Said, 18 December, 1956. General Stockwell is on the right.

United Nations Secretary-General U Thant with Ambassador Gunnar Jarring.

4. *UN Troops controlling a demonstration in the Gaza strip, 10 March, 1957*

5. *Military observer operation in the Suez Canal Sector, January, 1969*

functioning of UNEF) and with those countries providing contingents for UNEF.

In the meantime the Commander of UNEF was under great pressure from the Egyptian military command to evacuate his positions along the Demarcation Line. To all demands he turned a diplomatic but deaf ear, repeating that he could only change his troop dispositions on orders from the Secretary-General. On 17 May the Egyptian army began infiltrating into the demilitarized zone, establishing itself between the observation posts of the Yugoslav contingent at the southern end of the line. In some cases they forced the Yugoslav sentries out of their posts and occupied them themselves; though more than once the Yugoslavs refused to leave and shared their posts with the intruders. But over the succeeding days the United Arab Republic stepped up its efforts to neutralize the effectiveness of UNEF. Its troop movements into the forward areas continued and the interference with UNEF's dispositions progressively increased. UNEF, without a mandate to use force to resist this take-over, were powerless to do anything—and even had they had such a mandate their strength was such as to make resistance unrealistic. From the time that President Nasser and his government withdrew their acceptance of its presence, UNEF was a 'dead duck', and was in no viable position to remain. Its job was done and it had no further part to play in staving off a Middle East conflict—the United Arab Republic was steering a collision course with Israel and no amount of procrastination was likely to deter her. By now UNEF's authority was being disregarded everywhere from the Gaza Strip to Sharm el Shekh. It was clear that UNEF had served its turn and it was with a sense of relief that General Rikhye and his Force received orders from the Secretary-General on the night of 18 May to begin its withdrawal on the next day. The instructions directed that the withdrawal would be orderly and at a pace dictated by the availability of transport by air, sea and land, to Port Said. All this of course depended upon the United Arab Republic's full co-operation, which at this particular moment was affected by its own military requirements and which later was to become virtually non-existent in the heat of battle.

The Canadians were the first to go. This was not by design but through necessity. The Canadian Government had reacted forcibly against Nasser's decision and Prime Minister Lester Pearson had made his feelings very plain. This had angered Nasser, who accused Canada of having been the procrastinator in the departure of UNEF. On 27 May he called for the immediate withdrawal of the Canadian forces in UNEF and gave them 48 hours to leave Egypt; warning that the Egyptian people were incensed by Canada's hostility and that he could no longer guarantee the safety of her soldiers on Egyptian soil. In the event the Canadians' withdrawal, though hurried, went unmolested; very different to that of the remaining contingents. With the Canadians' departure UNEF was deprived of its logistic and air support and had the Force been remaining it would have been necessary to replace them to enable the Force to remain functional.

General Rikhye's plan was to phase his withdrawal so that UNEF would finally withdraw from the Gaza Strip on 6 June, though the unavailability of commercial transport made it unlikely that the last troops would have sailed from Port Said before the end of that month. What he did not know was that Israel had selected 5 June for D-Day. During the fortnight following the receipt of the withdrawal order, the remaining contingents of UNEF had been concentrating first in theirs platoon and then company camps. By 5 June all but the Indians were concentrated in contingent camps. Half the Yugoslavs had already left for home and the advance party and baggage of the Swedish contingent were on their way to Port Said; their main body was due to leave that night.

Immediately the fighting started the Force Commander

ordered the complete concentration of the Indians, but this was not possible because one company guarding the airfield was by then cut off from the rest of the battalion. The Brazilian's camp at Rafah was also cut off from the main force for some days. General Rikhye had selected the sand dunes and beaches near Gaza as safe for the concentration and embarkation of his Force. He managed to persuade the local military authorities to remove their own troops from the area; a wise strategy, since at no time during the fighting did the Israelis shell it, and those who had managed to find refuge there were safe. This could not be said for the rest, the Indians particularly suffering heavy casualties before they were evacuated. During the six days of fighting 14 Indian soldiers were killed and 20 wounded (the only other casualties recorded were 1 Brazilian soldier killed and 1 wounded). Three of the Indians were killed and 2 wounded on 6 June when UNEF headquarters came under heavy Israeli mortar fire and shelling. This resulted in the virtual destruction of the Force's external radio links. Rikhye was unable to communicate with New York. Nor was he able to pass messages via UNTSO in Jerusalem because it too had suffered the impact of a Jordanian attack and its headquarters and staff were temporarily in the hands of their attackers. A last dramatic message from its radio room had been received by the UN Force headquarters in Cyprus reporting fighting in the compound outside, that the Jordanian army was in control of most of the headquarters building and that any moment it was expected that communications with the outside world would be cut; moments later the station went off the air. No sooner had this intelligence been relayed to New York than Cyprus picked up a morse message from General Rikhye. It was in truth an SOS giving the news that his headquarters and units were under heavy fire from the Israeli army, that his main radio communications had been destroyed and that he only had this short-range link left, that he was suffering casualties and could anything be done about stopping the shelling and mortaring. Something was done,* and a message was got to General Yitzhak Rabin, the Chief of Staff of the Israel Defence Forces, explaining UNEF's plight; shortly afterwards the shelling ceased.

On the same day an Indian supply column and one of its companies were attacked within minutes of each other. The convoy returning from Rafah was attacked by aircraft, tanks and machine guns; 5 soldiers were killed and a number wounded. It is difficult to explain this seemingly wanton act of murder by the Israeli army. It is alleged by Israel that the army believed that UNEF had gone and therefore these were abandoned UN vehicles being used by the enemy. If the story given by survivors in Cyprus later is true, the tanks were passing the convoy in the opposite direction and as they passed they sprayed each vehicle with machine gun fire. It is difficult to understand why the identity of the Indians was not immediately apparent. It was in similar circumstances that the Indian company was caught in the path of an Israeli tank advance. Taking cover in trenches only recently occupied by troops of the United Arab Republic, they were mistaken for fedayeen and they too suffered casualties. Later in the day when UAR units started mortaring an Israeli force from close to the Indian battalion's camp, counter-mortar fire killed 3 and wounded 14 Indians. Finally, on this black day for the Indian contingent, an officer evacuating 2 wounded soldiers, was killed with his charges when their vehicle was blown-up by a road mine. An attempt to withdraw the contingent to the safety of the beach failed because of the heavy shelling.

* The author was at the time acting in command of the UN Force in Cyprus (UNFICYP). Immediately on receipt of Rikhye's message, he rang up the Israel Ambassador in Nicosia, a personal friend. The Ambassador promised to get a message off at once and was true to his word. General Rabin received the message and took immediate action. It was another two years before the author met the man whose life he had indirectly preserved.

From 7 June onwards UNEF suffered no more attacks. The battle had passed them by, but it was senseless to contemplate a withdrawal from Port Said for that part of the Force still in the Gaza area. The Swedish contingent's advance party, which had left by train on 4 June, had got through to the port eventually after having had to leave the train on the east side of the Canal. With the UAR army in full retreat it was unlikely that UNEF could expect any help from that direction.

Soon after the fighting had begun, General Rikhye had cabled the Secretary-General to arrange emergency evacuation by ship from the Gaza beaches. This embarkation point proved unsuitable and an attempt to use Gaza port itself, though acceptable to Israel, was frustrated by continued sniper action around the port area. Eventually it was Israel who facilitated the departure of UNEF. She made available the new port of Ashoda, just north of Gaza, and provided buses to bring the troops to it. The Force left Ashoda on 17 June in three charter ships bound for Cyprus, from whence most of the contingents flew back home. Their last few days in Gaza had been difficult. Their food was nearly gone, Gaza was without water or electricity and sanitation arrangements were breaking down. But despite all their tribulations they did not lack in morale when they arrived in Cyprus.

This tragic end to what had been a remarkably successful effort at peacekeeping was an unjust reward for those countries who had borne the burden of the task for more than ten years. The blame does not lie on their shoulders. Nor does the blame lie on the shoulders of the Secretary-General, though there are many who are only too ready to make him the scapegoat for what they call his premature and precipitous withdrawal of the Force. The fact that the Force had lost its operational value once the consent of the host country had been withdrawn is a factor ignored or not appreciated by these critics. From that moment, UNEF had no more rights under the terms of the Status of

Force Agreement, which was in a way its passport to freedom of action and freedom of movement. The only reason for delaying the withdrawal would have been if there had been a chance of Nasser changing his mind, but after his rejection of U Thant's appeal, there was no reason to suppose that he would reverse his decision. During the hard bargaining between Nasser and Hammarskjöld that preceded the former's acceptance of the Force on Egyptian territory in the first place, the period of its stay was obviously discussed. Following the announcement of the agreement on 12 November, 1956, Colonel Hakem, the then Director-General of the Egyptian Information Department, announced that it had been accepted by the Secretary-General that UNEF should withdraw immediately whenever the Egyptian Government requested it to do so. The following day a similar statement was made over Radio Cairo.

These statements did not necessarily give an accurate interpretation of what was actually agreed, but there is Hammarskjöld's own aide-memoire* of 5 August, 1957, which at least confirms that the deployment of UNEF was delayed due to a difference of opinion over Egypt's insistence on her right to request the withdrawal of UNEF at any time. Hammarskjöld's view, expressed in his aide-memoire, was that having requested and accepted UN assistance, it was incumbent upon the Egyptian Government not to call for the Force's withdrawal before it had completed the task for which it had been authorized by the General Assembly; and that since there could well be differing views held at the time on whether or not the task had been fulfilled, any request for the Force's withdrawal should be a matter for discussion. It would appear that this viewpoint prevailed and formed the basis on which President Nasser agreed to the presence of UNEF in Egypt, since it was two days later that the Force began to arrive in Egypt. Dag Hammarskjöld

* United Nations Peacekeeping 1946–67. Documents and Commentary: The Middle East. Rosalyn Higgins, pp. 363–366.

admits in his aide-memoire that he recognized 'that there was an element of gambling involved which I felt I simply had to take in view of the danger that further delays might cause Egypt to change its mind, accept volunteers and throw our approaches overboard.'

It is not recorded what the final undertaking was that the Egyptian Government agreed to. There is talk of 'a piece of paper' (never produced) which was said to contain a firm agreement by President Nasser that any request by Egypt for the withdrawal of UNEF would first be referred to the General Assembly. Certainly Dag Hammarskjöld makes no such claim, but simply states that at the end of the interchange of communications between himself and the Egyptian Government, 'Egypt gave green lights for the arrival of the troops, thus, in fact, accepting my stand and letting it supercede their own. . . .' Moreover, in an earlier aide-memoire* in November 1956, a few days after UNEF had become operational, the Secretary-General reported that 'the Government of Egypt declares that, when exercising its sovereign rights on any matter concerning the presence and functioning of UNEF, it will be guided, *in good faith*, by its acceptance of the General Assembly resolution. . . .'†

As Secretary-General U Thant pointed out after UNEF's withdrawal in 1967, this expression of good faith was never defined. It should also be realized that the aide-memoire of 5 August, quoted above, is a private document which was never made available to the General Assembly or to the Advisory Committee, nor communicated to the Government of Egypt. It is not anywhere on the official files of the United Nations and therefore has no official significance; it is purely a private paper

---

* A/3375. Report of Sec.-Gen. on presence and functioning in Egypt of UNEF: 20 November 1956.

† The resolution that established UNEF in order to secure and supervise the cessation of hostilities.

and as such could not affect the basis for the presence of UNEF on Egyptian soil.

This cloud of mystery that envelops the terms on which UNEF was finally accepted by Nasser may one day be dispelled; until then, no doubt, the controversy will continue over the rights and wrongs of U Thant's decision to order the withdrawal without first referring the question to the Security Council or the General Assembly. It is his view and it is one that can well be substantiated on procedural grounds, that the decision squarely rested with the Secretary-General after consultation with the Advisory Committee on UNEF, specifically set up by the General Assembly for consultation regarding such matters. Procedurally it was for the Committee to determine whether or not the question should be brought to the attention of the General Assembly. In the event the Committee did not so decide. In any case, under the terms of the 'Uniting for Peace' Resolution, the General Assembly, while enabled to establish the Force, had no powers to continue its operation counter to the wishes of the 'host' country, Egypt. So far as the Security Council was concerned, it had disagreed in the first place to the establishment of UNEF and it was therefore more than likely that it would have disagreed over its withdrawal— and in the words of U Thant 'would have complicated and exacerbated the situation, and, far from relieving the Secretary-General of the responsibility for the decision to be taken, would have made the decision much more difficult to take'.

The division of opinion on the procedural action taken will continue to be debated, but the underlying factor is that UNEF became inoperative and unable to fulfil its mandate the moment that the Egyptian Government withdrew its approval. So long as UN peacekeeping operations are mounted and peace forces are deployed on the basis of request or consent by the host country, the uncertainty of tenure will remain; but this is the risk that a peaceable intervention, as distinct from an enforcement action, will always run. However, the sudden change of heart by the host country resulting in a demand for the instant withdrawal of a UN Force must be insured against in future— not only in the interests of international peace, but also as a safeguard to the safety of the Force itself. Clearly a notice period is necessary and should be insisted upon as part of the arrangement with the host country. It should not be too short but should permit enough time for negotiations to take place with a view to persuading the host country to reconsider its decision, or, if that fails, to allow time in which other possible arrangements could be made for a UN presence in the area. In the final analysis such a notice would provide for an orderly and safe withdrawal of the Force. There seems no reason why an undertaking of this kind should in any way deny the host country the options of its sovereignty. It is to be hoped that were a new Force to be established in the Middle East to supervise and maintain peace, such an undertaking would be made by both the United Arab Republic and Israel; for this time such a Force would need to be acceptable to both sides if it were to have any measure of success. Looking at it cynically, the United Arab Republic might be less inclined another time to call for the immediate withdrawal of a second UNEF, in view of the hammer blow she received from the Israeli army when she did so before.

CHAPTER 3

Congo 1960-1964

I

The Congo is comparable in size to north-west Europe, a matter of 100,000 square miles at a conservative estimate. Distances between main communication centres are considerable, with the city of Leopoldville, the Republic's capital, and Elisabethville, the provincial capital of Katanga, as far apart as Paris and Athens. Viewed in these terms, the immensity of the United Nations peacekeeping operation can better be appreciated. It is accurately described as being the most difficult and complex of all the UN operations, during which 126 UN soldiers were killed and 138 were wounded.* The policing of such a vast area presented the UN Force (*Organisation des Nations Unies au Congo*—ONUC) with a stupendous task of organization and control; a task which would have daunted any other international group and made it hesitate to undertake such a responsibility. The very nature of the size and variety of the Force's heterogenous composition begat untold difficulties. The extended duration of the operation placed great pressure and strain on the contributing countries, particularly those with small professional armies.

Books have been written by senior officers and officials who were present in the Congo condemning its inefficiency and lack of effectiveness. Criticism alone, however justified, is of little value; but linked to constructive thought and recommendation, it can be of importance. Too much of the Congo literature lacks either. To expect a politico-military operation of the Congo type, mounted in the *ad hoc* fashion that has been the keystone of such operations, to be anything but a qualified success would

* A further 109 died accidentally or from natural causes.

be wholly unrealistic; but simply to underline its deficiencies without suggesting remedies helps no one. The UN operation in the Congo was the first of its kind and, because of the intricacies of the political situation, the lack of experience and the extremes of military preparedness, it was not surprising that there should have been considerable teething troubles in its evolution. But despite its shortcomings, the Congo operation, when studied in its proper perspective, did accomplish much. Looked at in the context of the direct and indirect achievements of the UN presence, no one could fairly describe it as being 'the

failure of a mission'. Non-viable in many ways maybe, but succeeding to a definite degree in the task for which it was provided.
Expensive, yes; long-lasting, yes; uneconomic in manpower,
yes; and there are many other entries on the debit side of the
ledger, commensurate with the fundamental organization and
mounting of the operation. But against them, two positive factors stand out, and here I quote two eminent authorities to
support my opinion. Mongi Slim of Tunisia, formerly his country's representative on the Security Council at the beginning of
the Congo operation and later Foreign Secretary, speaking at
Columbia University in 1963, said in reference to the Congo,
'much controversy arose on the merits of such operations, with
many pros and cons. But what can be asserted beyond any
doubt is that the UN presence prevented the cold war from
settling in the Congo, that the unity of the Congo was re-
established thanks in large measure to the UN efforts, and that
the UN helped to avoid an impending chaos that threatened
peace and security not only in the Congo but in the whole
African continent'. And in the words of Britain's Mr Philip
Noel-Baker, Member of Parliament and Nobel Peace prize-
winner, 'the Congo to-day probably has the most stable and
well-founded administrative machinery of government of any
in Africa'; an almost incredible fact when one remembers the
anarchy and bloodshed that prefaced the UN intervention in
1960. There are good reasons for saying that the Congo bene-
fitted from that intervention.

2

The Congo received its independence on 1 July, 1960, but
fifteen days later UN military assistance began to arrive in
answer to a call for help from the government of the newly-
created republic. It is doubtful if there has been a similar instance in history when third-party intervention of such a kind

has followed so quickly upon decolonization. A week after the ex-Belgian colony had raised its national flag of independence, anarchy had broken loose and was already beyond the control of the Government. It was expected that tribal clashes would follow independence, with one or other of the tribes striving to establish its ascendancy. So, when it happened, nobody was particularly surprised, but the mutiny of the Congolese army, the *Force Publique*, five days after independence, had not been expected.

It is difficult to understand why the discontent in the ranks of the *Force Publique* over pay and promotion, which had been apparent before independence, had been disregarded. It seems that the Belgians had done little to prepare the Congo's military forces for responsibilities of command after they had handed over—presumably they assumed that many of them would be invited to remain at their posts and become the army's backbone for some years to come. The chief cause of dissatisfaction among the African soldiers was that their chances of promotion were limited to the rank of warrant officer. Coupled with their general dissatisfaction over pay and conditions, the seeds of revolt were well sown and it only needed the appointment of Belgian officers to military staff posts after independence to set the fuse alight. Possibly a little more foresight on the part of the Belgian General Staff might have diverted the holocaust that followed, but then the trustees of other colonial territories have made similar mistakes.

On the night of 5/6 July, the *Force Publique* in Camp Leopold II, outside Leopoldville, mutinied. They disarmed and confined their European officers. Some of these were later released, but others were shot. The mutiny spread to other camps, but there was very little fighting at the beginning. Despite the apparent placidity of the revolt, all efforts by the Government to bring it to a halt were unsuccessful. Promises were given to the mutineers that their demands on pay and conditions would be met, but these had little or no effect. 'Until', the mutineers said, 'there is full Africanization of the officer ranks the revolt will continue'. Shortly the soldiers were joined by the *gendarmerie*.

From the outset it appeared that the wrath of the mutineers was directed against the Belgian and European residents. A subsequent evaluation by the Belgian Government expressed the opinion that a general order had been given to the mutineers to 'humiliate as deeply as possible their former European masters but to avoid accusations of massacre from world opinion'. Whatever the motives or desires of the mutineers, humiliation and genocide went hand in hand. Numbers of Europeans were murdered, others were simply never heard of again; atrocities of every kind were committed, reminiscent of the worst outrages of the Indian Mutiny. A Belgian Government report published at the end of July 1960 cited 291 cases of white women and children being raped in the four weeks since the mutiny began. Of these victims, some reported having been raped twelve, fifteen and even twenty times; some were raped so frequently that they could not remember how many times. Often it was a case of a mother submitting on condition that her daughter went unmolested; others were forced to submit under the visible threat of the bayoneting of their children or of themselves.

It was not surprising that, when the news of these atrocities and the abominable savagery began to filter through, panic spread among those who had so far escaped and a mass exodus started with hundreds fleeing across the river to Brazzaville in the former French Congo. By the morning of 8 July it was estimated that more than 3,000 European refugees had fled.

The mutiny was still spreading and violence was increasing. Among the victims in these early days was the Italian vice-consul in Katanga who was dragged from his car in Elisabethville and shot. With no positive signs of the Congo Government being able to control the situation, the Belgian Government sent army reinforcements from Belgium and followed them with a build-up of strength over the ensuing weeks. The Belgian army in the Congo had so far not gone into action against the mutineers, but now it did, on the grounds that it had the lives of Belgians to protect. The flow of refugees out of the country continued unabated.

On 11 July two significant things happened. Prime Minister Lumumba appealed to the United Nations for military assistance, primarily to help in the reorganization of the Congolese army, and to collaborate in re-establishing order and public security. At almost the same time, the provincial head of Katanga Province, Moise Tshombe, declared Katanga an independent state and announced its secession from the Congo. This action by Tshombe had no legal foundation and, since the greatest proportion of the Congo's industrial wealth, copper, lay within its provincial boundaries, the act of secession represented not only an unconstitutional act but also the illegal confiscation of the national wealth. In his declaration Tshombe blamed the disintegration of law and order in the Congo on communist influence which the present Government was only too willing to promote; but Katanga, he said, could not lend itself to such schemes and for this reason it would establish an independent state.

With fighting still going on between the mutineers and Belgian troops and no signs yet of military assistance from the United Nations, Lumumba turned to President Nkrumah of Ghana. Nkrumah obliged by sending his British Chief of Staff, Major-General Alexander, to Leopoldville and promised a military follow-up.

In the meantime the Security Council had passed a resolution calling for the withdrawal of Belgian troops from the Congo and authorizing the Secretary-General to furnish the Congolese Government with all necessary military assistance—along with the technical assistance that already had been promised, until the Congo's own security forces were in a position to deal fully with their responsibilities. (The USSR surprisingly did not veto the resolution, but only tried to obtain the immediate withdrawal of the Belgian army. This manoeuvre did not succeed, essentially because the UK delegate, Mr (now Sir) Harold Beeley, pointed to the dangers of leaving a vacuum between the Belgians' departure and the arrival of the first UN contingents). The next day Tshombe declared that under no circumstances would he allow UN troops to enter Katanga territory, insisting that the Belgian troops that had come to his aid should remain.

3

The first UN contingents (Tunisian and Ghanaian), flying in United States military aircraft, reached Leopoldville on 15 July, just four days after Lumumba's request for assistance and two days after the Security Council's resolution. From then onwards the build-up was gradual but sustained. By the end of July the UN Force totalled more than 10,000 and was later to increase to 20,000, the strongest it was to be at any one time. Quickly following on the heels of the Tunisians and Ghanaians were contingents from Morocco, Ethiopia, Sweden, Guinea, Ireland, and Liberia. On 18 July, General von Horn (Sweden), the Chief of Staff of the UN Supervisory Truce Organization in Palestine, arrived to take command. The Secretary-General appointed Hr Sture Linner, a Swedish businessman, as Chief of Operations and Sir Alexander McFarquhar of Britain as Special Adviser for Civilian Operations.

It is important to understand the politico-military control of these UN operations, particularly since it was different in the case of both Egypt and Cyprus. In the Congo the Chief of Operations was a civilian and the Force Commander was responsible to him for the military direction. In addition, there

. Members of the Indonesian contingent of the UN Force in the Congo carrying
ut military exercises outside their headquarters at Coquilhatville, November, 1960.

. A soldier of the UN Force in the Congo takes cover behind an armoured vehicle—
Elisabethville, 14 December, 1961.

8. *UN Troops in Cyprus; from left—Swedish, British, Canadian, Danish, Finnish, Irish.*

9. *Yugoslav soldiers of the UN Observation Mission in Yemen (UNYOM), June, 1963.*

was Dr Ralph Bunche, who was the Secretary-General's Special Representative in the Congo. It cannot be said to have been a very satisfactory arrangement and it is good that the lesson was learnt in time to improve upon it in Cyprus. One only has to read von Horn's book *Soldiering for Peace* to understand the personality friction that existed between the senior soldiers and civilians in the early days of the Congo operation and to what extent it damaged the mutual working harmony so essential to an operation of this kind. The point needs to be understood that the conduct of the Congo operation (as was also the case in Egypt and Cyprus) rested with the Secretary-General—a responsibility vested in him by the decision of the Security Council. It is therefore for him to decide the delegation of field command, and since the United Nations is a political, not a military, organization, it is understandable that Dag Hammarskjöld should have retained the civilian control in the field and placed the military in support. Understandable maybe, but the meld did not work and much disagreement was generated. It will be seen when we come to consider the Cyprus operation how the chain of command was improved. But the difficulties in the Congo did not end with the clash of personalities between senior officials; the piecemeal build-up of the staff over a period of months did not ease the already complex problems arising out of an operation of such magnitude.

Fighting was still in progress between the Belgians and the mutineers at Coquilhatville and Luluabourg and between the Baluba and Lulua tribes in Kasai province when the first elements of the UN Force arrived. It was important that it should establish itself quickly, so that the complete withdrawal of the Belgian army could be effected. This withdrawal was at the insistence of the Security Council who considered that the continued presence of the Belgian troops in the Congo only exacerbated the situation. On the other hand, the Belgian Government were reluctant to comply with the Security Council's demand

4

until the UN presence was sufficiently established to protect the lives of their nationals.

So far no UN troops had been sent into Katanga, but on 2 August, 1960, the Secretary-General announced that the first units would start moving in on the 6th. Tshombe, who alleged that the first he knew of the statement was from a local newspaper, immediately ordered general mobilization of Katanga's armed forces to resist the entry of UN troops. His resolve to take armed action to contest any attempt by the UN to station a force in Katanga found favour with the *Association des Enterprises du Katanga*, an associate body of the sixty-seven most important business concerns in the province. Their reason for criticizing the Secretary-General's intention was that it would paralyze the economy. More than once in the Congo (and the Congo has not been the only case) the vested interests of big business succeeded in hindering and frustrating the United Nations in its peacekeeping efforts.

Because of Tshombe's reaction, the Secretary-General delayed moving the troops until the Security Council had had an opportunity to consider the position—on the grounds that a Katangese armed confrontation would inevitably mean that the UN would have to use force to obtain entry and this would be against the principles under which contributing nations had agreed to provide contingents. On 9 August the Security Council gave Dag Hammarskjöld the support he looked for, declaring that the entry of UN troops into Katanga was necessary to the full implementation of the original Security Council resolution. Eventually the entry was achieved in a peaceful fashion on 12 August, when Hammarskjöld himself arrived in Elisabethville, along with 300 Swedish troops. None of this pleased Lumumba, who accused the Secretary-General of connivance with Tshombe against the Congolese Government, in that he had forestalled the latter from taking military action against Katanga. Lumumba insisted that the UN's role in the Congo was not one of neutralism but one of support for the Government and that it should place all its available resources at the Congo Government's disposal—i.e. that the UN Force should be used by it to subdue Katanga. In its resolution of 14 July, the Security Council authorized the Secretary-General to provide 'such military assistance as may be necessary until (Congolese) national security forces may be able in the opinion of the Government to meet fully their tasks'. Although certain aspects of the ONUC mandate were to change later in respect of Katanga itself, the basis on which the UN intervened did not include armed assistance in dealing with internal disorders which did not threaten international peace. These remained the concern of the Congolese Government.

This misapprehension of the Force's role and of its mandate was not confined to Lumumba alone—others were to share this misconception and, as with Lumumba, it was to strain relations between the Congolese Government and the United Nations for a large part of the time that ONUC remained on Congolese soil, and was to be the cause of a number of hostile attacks against UN soldiers and civilians.

The first of these occurred at Leopoldville airport on 15 August, when Congolese soldiers and *gendarmerie* surrounded it and began interfering with UN troop movements. In one instance they detained some Canadian army signallers, Moroccan civilians and Indian aircrew, beat them up with rifle butts and ill-treated other Canadian passengers. A sorry side of this tale was that members of the Ghanaian contingent who witnessed the incident did little to provide protection for their unfortunate UN colleagues. The subsequent protest that went to Nkrumah appears to have been lightly regarded and the blame for the lack of reaction on the part of the Ghanaian soldiers was placed firmly at the door of the UN by General Alexander, in whose opinion it was the fault of the ambiguity of the directives on the use of force. This seems a poor excuse for doing nothing to save one's comrades. Alexander's attitude underlines a basic tendency among many professional soldiers to find difficulty in adapting to the concept of peaceable intervention and self-defence as practised in UN peacekeeping operations. On 18 August the UN forces regained control of the airport and retained it thereafter.

A second incident concerned two UN security guards who were detained by the Congolese army and held in the guard-room of the Prime Minister's house. In an effort to secure their release, Major-General Indar Rikhye, Military Adviser to Dag Hammarskjöld who was temporarily in Leopoldville, and Mr George Ivan Smith, an Australian and a member of Dr Bunche's staff, went to the Prime Minister's house. On arrival they were halted by the sentry at the gate and refused entry until Ivan Smith barked at him, 'Don't you know a General when you see one? Stand to attention! Present arms!'—the soldier sprang to his bidding and Rikhye and Ivan Smith passed on. On arrival at the guardroom, Ivan Smith once again called upon the ser-geant of the guard to pay due courtesies to the 'illustrious Indian General'. The sergeant, too astonished to demur, turned out the guard and while General Rikhye inspected it, Ivan Smith slipped into the guardroom and came out with the two very frightened security men whom he bundled into the car. Having succeeded in releasing the men, a courtesy call was paid on the Prime Minister.

4

At the end of August, Bunche returned to his post as Permanent Under-Secretary for Political Affairs at the United Nations and was replaced by Rajeshwar Dayal, hitherto Indian High Com-missioner in Pakistan and a former member of the UN observer group in the Lebanon. At the beginning of September the last

Belgian troops, except for some technicians, left for home. The fighting among the tribes continued and the Congolese army moved into Kasai province to deal with the rebellious Balubas, who suffered cruelly at its hands. Despite the savagery of the 'civil war', it was the responsibility of the central government and the army to maintain law and order and it was not for ONUC physically to intervene. But this was not the only area of conflict at that time. For some weeks relations between President Kasavubu and Prime Minister Lumumba had grown increasingly strained. Now they were to break down altogether.

On 5 September Kasavubu dismissed Lumumba as Prime Minister on the grounds that he was leading the country into civil war and replaced him by Joseph Ileo, then President of the Senate. Lumumba immediately responded by dismissing Kasavubu from the Presidency for 'being a traitor to the State'. He went to the radio station in Leopoldville and denounced Kasavubu in similar terms and followed this with a further broadcast the next day. He was backed by his Cabinet, but the Chamber of Representatives invalidated both declarations. So each remained President and Prime Minister respectively. For reasons of public order the radio station, which was now under the control of the UN, was closed, as was the airport to avoid any possible intervention from outside. These closures, on the orders of Andrew Cordier who was acting as Hammarskjöld's personal representative until Dayal arrived, were hotly criticized later, particularly by the USSR, as an act of intervention totally outside the terms of reference set down in the Security Council's resolution. When later Lumumba, accompanied by twenty of his soldiers, tried to storm into the radio station and was prevented by a platoon of Ghanaians under the command of a British lieutenant, George Short, the USSR accused 'this extremist of a coloniser' of having threatened Lumumba with his revolver. Lumumba was Russia's man in the battle for power. Ghana also took sides with Lumumba, and in so doing alienated herself from his opponents, President Kasavubu and General Mobutu. Because of ONUC's occupation of the radio station and closure of the airport, the UAR withdrew its parachute battalion serving with the Force in protest against 'this flagrant violation of the Congo's sovereignty and the independent and territorial integrity of the country'; in her opinion ONUC had exceeded its mandate.

On 12 August Lumumba was arrested on Ileo's orders but almost immediately induced his military guards to release him. Reappearing in the capital with an escort of soldiers, he once again attempted to broadcast from the radio station. Though both the airport and the radio station were reopened the next day 'to peaceful traffic', Cordier made it clear that it was not because of any external pressures. It had never been meant as anything but a temporary emergency at a tense period. The past few days had been quiet and therefore the restrictions had been lifted.

The power struggle continued and when General Mobutu announced on 14 September that the Army was taking over the situation became yet more confused. Mobutu was 30 and had risen to the rank of sergeant-major in the *Force Publique* when he retired in 1956. He then took a course at the Institute of Social Studies in Brussels. Returning to the Congo, he took up a journalistic career; then joined Lumumba's government as a secretary of state, and on the outbreak of the mutiny he was appointed Army Chief of Staff. His declaration coincided with his appointment as Commander-in-Chief in place of General Lundula, whom Kasavubu had sacked. His first act was to suspend the political leaders and appoint a 'college of high commissioners' to take over the duties of government and parliament. The commissioners were Congolese graduates and students called home from their studies abroad. This 'college' was never recognized by the UN as being the authoritative body of government in the Congo; as far as the UN was concerned, only the constitutionally-elected government could be so recognized. The college of commissioners eventually faded out after about six months.

With Lumumba still living in his official residence, and so far as he and his supporters were concerned, very much still the Prime Minister, with Kasavubu and Ileo still carrying on their activities despite the decree suspending them, and the Senate continuing its sessions in competition with the college of commissioners, and with Tshombe in Katanga refusing to be a party to the follies of the central government, the political scene in the Congo was totally confused. With no mandate to intervene, the UN kept clear of this constitutional fracas, but its effects of course made the Force's task much more difficult.

Shortly after Mobutu's announcement, Lumumba made an abortive attempt to regain control. He hoped for support from the soldiers, but they proved hostile and he was forced to take refuge in the officers' mess of the Ghanaian contingent which was immediately surrounded by Congolese soldiers intent on assassinating him. On the orders of Mobutu he was allowed to leave under escort, brought to Leopoldville and placed under arrest, from which he almost immediately escaped and went into hiding.

Mobutu was particularly critical of the attitude of the Ghanaians and Guineans who, in his opinion, were actively supporting and protecting Lumumba. Mobutu, on 'assuming power', had ordered the embassies of all communist countries to close within forty-eight hours because of 'their potential threat of intervening in the internal affairs of the country'. Now his relations with the UN were to go through a worsening period. It did not help matters when the Guinean contingent commander gave a dinner in Lumumba's honour at which, incidentally, the latter had openly attacked the UN and its conduct of the operation. To say the least, this would seem to have been a tactless gesture on the part of the contingent commander, but it must be accepted that there existed a definite degree of partisanship among African contingents in the Congo, which was not surprising in view of the vested interests involved. Whatever the reasons, it did not help the UN image of impartiality which was so vital to the role that it had to play.

ONUC was not a 'happy mix' at this time, with its temperamental withdrawals and threats of withdrawal. At the beginning of 1961 there came what was called the 'Casablanca pull-out', when the UAR, Morocco, Ceylon and Guinea withdrew their contingents on the grounds of dissatisfaction with the UN's handling of the operation (basically because it would not involve itself more actively in the internal problems of law and order). Indonesia withdrew its contingent at the same time, but rejoined the Force later. These losses were immediately replaced either from other countries or through some of the existing member countries increasing their contribution. The end result made for a better-balanced force.

During October 1960, relations between Mobutu and the UN reached breaking-point, because of what he termed the UN's continued support of Lumumba and interference in the authorities' attempts to arrest him. Since the power struggle was still as undecided as ever, and since Lumumba was still constitutionally the Prime Minister, there was no legal substance to back Mobutu's claims, nor for him to make the arrest. Without a legal document of arrest the UN certainly could not permit Lumumba to be arrested. The UN were in the Congo at the request of the constitutionally-elected Government, to assist it in the re-establishment of national stability. Mobutu's act of declaration had in no way altered the position, for he had acted unilaterally and was not recognized as being anything other than the Commander-in-Chief of the Army. So the Ghanaian guard on the Prime Minister's residence remained—a security precaution that had been in force for some time for both the President and for Prime Minister.

Lumumba himself did not make things easier by periodically leaving his house unescorted to harangue people in the streets and cafés, but he seemed to command sufficient support to get away with it.

The month of November showed little improvement in the situation. Fighting still continued in Kasai province where 5,000 Baluba tribesmen, led by mercenary officers, including an Englishman, 'Captain Roberts' (a former 2nd Lieutenant in the British Army), had their advance checked by UN forces after they had defied the truce and burnt a number of villages. An Irish patrol was surrounded and ambushed by Balubas at Niemba in North Katanga when trying to remove a roadblock on 8 November. Lt Gleeson and 9 of the 11-man patrol were killed, the other 2 managing to escape, though wounded. This was the heaviest loss of life yet. It is believed that the Baluba tribesmen, who till then had allowed UN patrolling to pass unmolested, were on this occasion under the influence of drugs—'strong witchcraft' as they later admitted.

Towards the end of the month the Ghanaian embassy was attacked by troops of the Congolese army because the ambassador had not complied with an expulsion order issued by Mobutu. In the fighting 1 UN soldier of the Tunisian contingent guarding the embassy was killed and 8 others wounded. On the Congolese side 3 were killed, including the army's deputy Chief of Staff who was shot when trying to force an entry through the embassy cellar. In this incident the UN guard opened fire first—but this was justifiable in the circumstances since it was exercising its right to use force in self-defence. Reactions against the UN were immediate and, in the days following the funeral of the Congolese, 45 UN soldiers and civil staff were assaulted.

In the meantime a pro-Lumumba group had set itself up in power at Stanleyville, capital of Orientale province, with

Antoine Gizenga, the deputy Prime Minister, in charge. He was joined by General Lundula, ex-Commander-in-Chief, who had succeeded in escaping from Leopoldville. Lumumba was still in his house in the capital, but he too slipped out unnoticed and left Leopoldville by car. It was expected that he would go straight to Stanleyville, but instead he turned up in Kasai province. Mobutu's men went after him and on 1 December detained him at Port Francqui. From then on, his life must have been a nightmare. He was brought back to Leopoldville with 2 companions in the back of an open lorry, tied like a common felon, to the accompaniment of boos from the crowds along the way. First held prisoner in the army barracks at Thysville, he appears from later reports to have been consistently and methodically ill-treated. At the beginning of January 1961, he was transferred to Katanga, into the hands of his implacable enemy Tshombe. Here he was held until 10 February, in a farmhouse outside Elisabethville. Still subjected to systematic beatings, his physical condition was said to have been appalling. On 10 February it was reported that he and his 2 fellow prisoners had escaped by overcoming their guards, seizing their rifles and getting away in their car—a remarkable feat in the light of their alleged physical condition. Two days later, news came that all 3 had been captured and killed at an undisclosed village near Kolwezi. The official statement, to say the least, sounds improbable. The more likely truth is that Lumumba was killed by his captors. One story has it that a Katangese official had stabbed him to death with a bayonet that he had seized in a moment of temper from a guard. Another is that a European officer shot him out of pity—as if putting a wounded animal out of its misery. Whatever the truth, there is little doubt that Lumumba had been so brutally beaten-up during the period that he was a prisoner that he would have died shortly in any case.

The world-wide reaction to the news of Lumumba's death was strong and outspoken. ONUC was placed on full alert and empowered by the Security Council to use all methods possible to contain civil war—using force if necessary as a last resort. Tension ran very high for a time and during this period two major and serious clashes occurred between UN and Congolese troops. At Matadi on 3 March, a Sudanese company of 130, including a Canadian signal detachment, was attacked by 1,000 Congolese. The company held out for 2 days but was then forced to evacuate its position, losing 2 killed and 13 wounded with 15 more Sudanese and Canadians missing. It took 3 months of assiduous negotiation before the UN were successful in re-establishing a presence at Matadi.

Seven weeks later, at the end of April, 38 Ghanaian soldiers and 4 British and Swedish officers were killed at Port Francqui when their garrison was overrun by elements of the Congolese army. These were hazardous days for the UN Force with pro-Lumumbists indulging in a reign of terror.

Early in January, Major-General Sean McEown (later to become Chief of Army Staff of the Irish Army) had taken over as Force Commander from von Horn, who had returned to Palestine, and now in May another Irishman, Dr Conor Cruise O'Brien, took over as co-ordinator of UN activities in Katanga, following Rajeshwar Dayal who had resigned as Special Representative in order to return to his diplomatic duties in Pakistan. On the Congolese side, Cyrille Adoula replaced Ileo as Prime Minister in August and was to remain in office throughout the remainder of the emergency.

The story from here on largely concerns Katanga and its fight to remain seceded from the rest of the Republic. Peace had by no means been established in Kasai or Kivu provinces, where fighting and bloodshed continued, and Gizenga and the Lumumbists still exercised complete control over Elisabethville; only Leopoldville and Equator could be said to be under the control of the central government. But despite considerable difficulties and frequent attacks by marauding tribesmen against its widespread detachments, ONUC was managing to maintain order in the main centres of Kasai and Kivu and, to a degree, protect the European settlers in outlying communities from Lumumbist attacks, which were being particularly directed against them as part of a revenge campaign.

In Katanga tension was running high, and the influx of foreign mercenaries into the *gendarmerie*, far from being halted by the authorities, was on the increase. The Security Council's resolution to 21 February, 1961, called for the expulsion of all mercenaries from Katanga. Tshombe had so far disregarded the resolution, but on 28 August President Kasavubu demanded that it should be implemented. The very same day, UN troops occupied key points in Katanga and rounded up 512 European officers serving with the Katangese forces. An Irish guard was placed around the house of the Minister of Interior, Munongo, who was suspected of organizing 'a murder campaign against UN soldiers and civilians' (an attempt by O'Brien to have him suspended was not successful). Next day Tshombe capitulated to the demand for the expulsion of all mercenaries and he broadcast an endorsement to this effect; but as was so often the case with Tshombe, his public statements rarely matched up to his real intentions. It was not long before mercenaries appeared once again within the ranks of the Katangese forces, leading them against the UN and in raids into Kasai against central government troops.

'Rumpunch', the codename by which the operation of 21 February was known, provided only a temporary respite. The undertaking of the Belgian consul in Elisabethville to repatriate the many Belgians among the mercenaries detained was not exactly fulfilled and in the event hardly more than half the number finally left Katanga.

The UN Command, in initiating direct military action against the Katangese, might be said to have acted outside their mandate, as prescribed by the Security Council's resolutions. But Operation Rumpunch was aimed at rounding-up the foreign mercenaries whose continued presence could be said to constitute an act of aggression against the authority of the central government. The occupation of the Post Office and radio station and the surrounding of Godefroid Munongo's house were less plausible actions but could be justified on the grounds that their purpose was to protect the Congo's territorial integrity. It was not many days before the deteriorating situation activated a bloodier and more ominous clash between ONUC and the Katangese.

Operation Morthor (Hindi for 'smash'), later described as Round One of ONUC's intervention to end the secession, began at 4 am on 13 September. It continued for eight days and it is estimated some 50 Katangese and 11 UN troops were killed. The operation followed a series of abortive attempts to get Tshombe to co-operate. The operation orders included the arrests of Tshombe and some of his senior ministers. In this ONUC was acting in close collaboration with Adoula's government which had issued the arrest warrants with which the UN Force was armed. The idea was to bring pressure to bear on Tshombe to agree to an end to secession. The plan backfired. Tshombe eluded arrest and escaped into hiding and only one of his ministers was apprehended. Fighting around the Post Office and radio station was heavy but eventually they fell to Indian troops. At one point on the first evening O'Brien announced to reporters that secession was at an end, despite the fact that Tshombe was still at large and the general situation was one of confusion.

Operation Morthor clearly failed in its purpose and was possibly the most ill-judged action of the whole Congo operation. Up to this point, the UN had adhered strictly to the Security Council resolution that there would be no interference in the political life of the Congo. Operations Rumpunch and Morthor had been a departure from the principle of that resolution, though they could be said to draw some justification from subsequent resolutions 'urging all possible measures to prevent civil war'. Had the second operation proved immediately successful and had it achieved all its objectives, including the detention of Tshombe and his ministers on the first day, then it is probable that secession would have ended and the UN would have been acclaimed for bringing the Katanga problem to a bloodless end. As it was, nothing like it was achieved. When on 20 September a cease-fire and truce were agreed, the terms of the truce provided for an exchange of prisoners, the return of the radio station, Post Office and other public buildings to Katangese control. Politically it was a return to the *status quo ante*, with the UN having nothing to show for its endeavours; in fact ONUC might be said to have received a military setback. During the operation a 200-strong company of Irish had been encircled by the Katangese and, greatly outnumbered, had been compelled to surrender after a tenacious resistance; in spite of the provisions of the truce of 20 September requiring the immediate exchange of prisoners, the luckless Irish were held captive until 25 October.

Dag Hammarskjöld had arrived in the Congo on 12 September. He had come at the request of the Congolese Government which was deeply concerned at the deterioration in the situation. Tshombe, who had escaped to Northern Rhodesia at the start of Operation Morthor, agreed to meet him at the Rhodesian town of Ndola, near the Katanga border. The Secretary-General left Leopoldville for Ndola in his personal aircraft *Albertina* on 18 September. The plane crashed when approaching Ndola airfield and Dag Hammarskjöld and his companions, all personal staff, were killed. Mystery still surrounds the disaster. Both the United Nations and the Northern Rhodesian Government mounted independent investigations into the causes of the crash and both ruled out sabotage, with the latter ascribing the blame to pilot's error. But there are those who were close to the Congo scene at the time who hold different views. 'Colonel' Jacques Duchemen, a French journalist who had been a military councillor of the Katangese Ministry of Defence since 1960, considers that Hammarskjöld was the victim of a 'stupidly banal accident' when an attempt engineered by Tshombe to kidnap him in the air went wrong. Duchemen's account has a James Bond flavour. He alleges that Tshombe got the idea from a newspaper describing a recent aerial hi-jacking. Thinking that by kidnapping and holding the Secretary-General as hostage he could achieve the complete humiliation of the United Nations and its withdrawal from Katanga, Tshombe hired a Belgian officer, carrying false papers, to get aboard the *Albertina* disguised as a UN sergeant. He was to hold up the pilot as they approached Ndola and order him to set course for Kolwezi inside Katangan territory. According to Duchemen's theory the attempt failed, the pilot refused to change course and put the aircraft into a sharp turn in order to throw the hi-jacker off balance, but in doing so touched the top of the trees with his wing-tip and crashed. Whether or not there is any truth in this 'account', certain facts do point to there being a different answer to that of 'pilot's error'. First, there *was* an extra body among the corpses which was never identified. Second, one of the victims had a bullet in his body. Third, no radio contact was made with the traffic-control tower after the pilot had notified it that he was preparing to descend for landing only ten minutes' flying time away. Fourth and finally, the plane is said to have circled over Ndola for almost another hour after the final radio contact.

There are others besides Duchemen who are not convinced by the accident verdict, for the same or similar reasons. Whatever the truth, Dag Hammarskjöld's death was an international tragedy and came at a time when he could ill be spared.

5

After Round One the situation in Katanga showed little improvement. Attacks on UN troops continued, both inside and outside Katanga. Probably the most horrifying of these was at Kindu in Kivu province where thirteen Italians, the aircrew of a UN transport plane, were brutally murdered by Congolese troops after they had been forcibly dragged from a Malaysian officers' mess. Afterwards their bodies were dismembered and parts sold in the local market for food.

Round One had caused an international furore and a number of member states, including Britain, deplored the action that had been taken to end the Katanga secession, claiming that ONUC had gone beyond its mandate. It is likely that, had Round One been successful, the outraged voices would have been somewhat muted. The protestations, however, were enough to decide O'Brien to submit his resignation and he departed from the Katanga scene on 1 December.

To counter the continued unrest and attacks on UN troops, U Thant, the newly-elected Secretary-General, authorized his officials in the Congo 'to take every measure possible' for the restoration of law and order and the UN's freedom of action in Elisabethville. At the same time Tshombe was warned that unless he regained control of his military forces, the UN would use force against them. Almost simultaneously with this directive, fighting broke out on the outskirts of Elisabethville when Katangese *gendarmerie* resisted Gurkha units' attempts to remove a roadblock.

Round Two lasted longer than its predecessor and it was a full two weeks before the fighting stopped. For the first time the troops had air support (ONUC had latterly been supplied with a small number of jet fighters and transport planes) and in the course of the fighting considerable damage was done to buildings, through mortaring and bombing. The total casualties recorded were 206 Katangese soldiers and 50 civilians killed against 25 UN soldiers killed. But Round Two also failed to achieve an end to secession and brought renewed criticism that the UN Force had gone beyond its declared principle of self-defence. U Thant denied this charge, citing the campaigns of violence and the setting up of roadblocks by Tshombe's *gendarmerie* to obstruct ONUC's freedom of movement as solid reasons for the Force taking the action that it did. By 21 December, when a truce was arranged, ONUC was in possession of about a third of the city. Under the terms of the truce (the Kitona Agreement), Tshombe undertook to recognize the indissoluble unity of the Republic, to recognize President Kasavubu as its Head of State, to recognize the authority of the central government over all parts of the Republic and to agree to the placing of the Katangese *gendarmerie* under the authority of the President. The next day, the Katanga cabinet declared itself incompetent to authorize President Tshombe to make the 'declaration' imposed upon him; and on 26 December fighting flared up again between the Katangese and the UN, as well as between Katangese and central government troops in the north of the province.

6

Nineteen sixty-one ended bleakly and the beginning of 1962 augured no better for the future. But the year to come was to be one of diplomatic exchanges aimed at bringing Tshombe to heel and at keeping him there. He had proved so often that his word was unreliable and he was to prove it yet again.

Early in 1962, Adoula and Tshombe met on a number of occasions to try and reach some understanding, but this series of talks broke down when Tshombe declined to participate any more because 'Adoula's attitude made dialogue impossible'. Nor was he apparently prepared to curb the attacks against UN soldiers in his province by his own *gendarmerie*. On one occasion in July, the *gendarmerie* instigated a demonstration of several thousand women and children in which 21 UN soldiers and a number of women were injured, with a woman and a boy being killed.

With the deadlock persisting, U Thant proposed a plan for a new federal constitution, to be implemented in four phases. It provided for the just division of revenues between the central government and provincial governments, a reconstitution of the central government to include representation from all political and provincial groups, and a unification of the Congolese armed forces. Adoula accepted the plan in principle; Tshombe intimated that he too was prepared to accept the terms, but at the same time he did not desist from rearming and strengthening his own armed forces; nor did he halt his air attacks against the central government forces in northern Katanga.

On 11 December the Secretary-General warned Tshombe that he intended going ahead with the implementation of his four-phase plan. Sixteen days later the final round in the battle of secession opened with a clash between the *gendarmerie* and Indian and Ethiopian units of ONUC. Tshombe accused the UN of being the first to open fire; he was immediately invited to see for himself that the firing had been all on one side—the Katangese. He saw and accepted the fact but totally failed to get the *gendarmerie* to desist; his orders for a cease-fire were disregarded. Since he had apparently lost control of his own soldiers, the UN took decisive action and by 28 December, after only thirty-six hours fighting, were in complete control in Elisabethville. The fighting had been heavy, with 75 Africans and 9 UN dead and many other Africans wounded. There followed the capture of the two towns of Kamina and Kipushi a day later. Round Three had been successful and received the plaudits of those who had so strongly condemned Rounds One and Two. Tshombe accused the UN soldiers of murder, rape and robbery—then disappeared along with his cabinet. In an ultimatum on 31 December, U Thant gave Tshombe two weeks in which to arrange the surrender of the Katangan air force to ONUC. All Katangese forces were to surrender their arms immediately and all mercenaries were to be expelled.

Mopping-up operations continued, culminating in the fall of Jadotville on the third day in the New Year. Tshombe remained in hiding until 8 January when he returned briefly to Elisabeth-ville, leaving it again two days later. Surprisingly, after ONUC's withdrawal in July, 1964, he succeeded in becoming the head of the Congo government. Helped once again by white mercenaries he attempted to govern by sheer force of arms. There followed bloody rebellion throughout the greater part of the Congo, resulting in worse bloodshed and fighting than during ONUC's four year presence. Tshombe's leadership came to an end in late 1965 when he was ousted by a coup led by Mobutu who took office in his place. Shortly afterwards Tshombe left the Congo for good. He was to die 'from a heart attack' (there were said to be eleven doctors' signatures on the death certificate!) in an Algerian prison in 1969, having been hi-jacked in his privately-chartered aircraft over the Mediterranean two years before and forced to land in Algeria. Poetic justice or just irony? It could have been both if Duchemen's story of the plot to kidnap Hammarskjöld that September night over Ndola in 1961 is the truth.

7

That is really the end of the ONUC story. Although fighting and unrest continued through 1963 and into 1964 when the final withdrawal of the UN Force was made, these were mainly

mention UN Killed 176 wounded 138

consolidating operations by government troops. Early in 1963 the size of ONUC was reduced to 5,000 and the emphasis was placed on the civilian rehabilitation effort. The secession of Katanga was ended on 15 January, 1963, twelve days after the end of Round Three. A day later law and order was restored in Stanleyville and the Lumumbist regime was brought to an end. Gizenga was held in protective custody for a time but was later set free as part of the general amnesty which was one of the requirements of U Thant's plan.

Once the internal strife abated, it was possible to increase the technical and development aid that was so vitally needed. The special agencies of FAO, WHO, UNESCO and UNDP had been working in the Congo since the beginning, but it was only in the later stages of the conflict that a full-scale assistance programme could be mounted. In 1963 $19,000,000 was provided by the UN for this programme. Much needed to be done. Rajeshwar Dayal, making his first report to the Secretary-General in September, 1960, on the situation facing the UN in the Congo, only too clearly illustrated the problem. He wrote,

'On attaining independence . . . the country would have been faced even in normal circumstances with many economic, social, political, military and administrative problems. . . . The almost complete lack of trained civil servants, executives and professional people among the Congolese and the striking absence of administrative and political experience . . . created a serious situation for the young republic. But this situation was made worse by a complete failure to arrange for any organized hand-over to the Congolese of the administrative machinery of government and essential services.'

When you add to that the fact that out of a population of 40,000,000 only 17 held university degrees, one can better estimate the unpreparedness of the Congolese people for self-government. Even the fairest-minded would say that the Belgians had much to answer for.

When the UN Force arrived it found a complete breakdown in public services, communications and supply, a serious health threat, a critical disruption in the economy of the country, total collapse of the social security and judicial systems and of the labour administration. Putting this jig-saw of broken pieces together again was a mammoth task, but it was done. In the concluding words of his report Dayal wrote, 'a great deal has been done in the face of insuperable odds . . . there is no doubt whatsoever that the UN presence has had a steadying effect on the situation'. In those early days of political confusion it was not surprising that UN actions, however impartial, were often criticized or condemned by one faction or another, but the civilian operation continued as best it could alongside that of the military and eventually took over when the military's responsibilities had come to an end.

The United Nations operation in the Congo showed up many deficiencies and weaknesses in the peacekeeping machinery. But it was a gigantic undertaking, and one never tried before. Of course there were failures during the four years—failures in command, in direction, in the conduct of the operations themselves. There was bitterness and rivalry within the Force. There was much that was wrong, but there was more that was right. It is the end result, the long-term and wider effects that are important and when one looks at these in the context of the Congo to-day, no one can deny that the overall result of the operation can be seen in terms of success, not failure.

CHAPTER 4

Cyprus: 1964-1971

I

On Christmas Eve, 1963, the growing antagonism existing between the Greek and Turkish Cypriots erupted into a
reign of terror which engulfed the whole of Cyprus, turning
Aphrodite's Island of Love into an island of hate. The schism
that it caused in the inter-communal relationship has yet to be
healed. Although the fighting ceased in 1967, the armed confrontation continues to this day largely because the obstinacy
of a relative few has prevented a settlement. All the indications
are that the great majority of both communities long to see an
end to the conflict, both politically and militarily, and a resump-
tion of peaceful co-existence—a situation that even now exists in
some parts of the island despite the continuing state of
disunity and hostility elsewhere.

Whether Greek or Turk, the Cypriots are a friendly, cheerful,
hospitable but volatile people, quick to anger and quick to
forget. It is therefore difficult to understand why the two communities cannot come to terms; perhaps were they to think of
themselves as Cypriots and not as Greeks and Turks it might
make things easier for them. Certainly there have been many
instances during the last seven years when natural affinities have
overcome the communal rift, and differences have been settled—
never more so than in those villages in Cyprus where Greeks
and Turks are living together, totally integrated and in harmony
despite the unsettled conflict between their two communities.

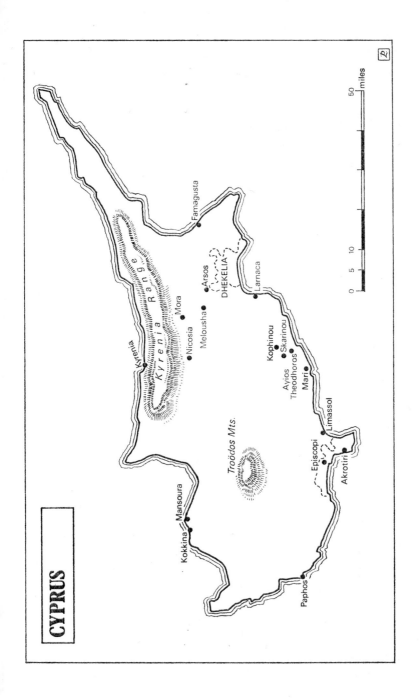

CYPRUS

Kokkina—Mansoura

Kyrenia
Kyrenia Range
Nicosia
Mora
Melousha
Arsos
DHEKELIA
Larnaca
Kophinou
Skarinou
Ayios Theodhoros
Mari
Troödos Mts.
Episcopi
Limassol
Akrotiri
Paphos
Famagusta

0 5 10   50
                 miles

2

Measuring only 3,500 square miles,* Cyprus lies in the eastern Mediterranean, 40 miles from the mainland of Turkey and 70 miles from Syria. Its population of just over half a million is 77% Greek and 18% Turkish, with the balance of 5% made up of Armenians, Maronites, British and others. The island came under British colonial administration in 1878 and remained so until 1960 when it achieved its independence and a self-governing constitution as a republic within the Commonwealth.† The years immediately preceding the granting of independence were unsettled. Under the leadership of Colonel Grivas, a guerrilla organization‡ carried on a four-year campaign of terrorism and intimidation which caused over 10,000 British soldiers to be brought to the island in an effort to control the internal security. It is a measure of the resistance offered by this comparatively small hard-core guerrilla movement and the control it had over the whole community that, in the end it was a political solution not a military victory that prevailed.

But when Cyprus attained independence in August 1960, she was destined to enjoy only three years of uneasy calm before the island was once again plunged into internal strife after the breakdown of her newly-formed constitution. That constitution had been too hurriedly put together, first in Zurich and later in London. The United Kingdom, Greece and Turkey, as the trustees of Cyprus' future, were bound by treaty to guarantee the independence of Cyprus; but the constitution lacked a soundly-based formula and it was not too long before this became self-evident. The Turkish Cypriots, ever mindful of their

---

* Approximately 140 miles long and 70 miles across at its widest point.

† The London-Zurich Agreements: February 1959.

‡ EOKA (Ethniki Organosis Kypriou Agoniston—National Organization of Cypriot Fighters).

minority status and the dangers of such a position, were suspicious and openly obstructive to anything the Greek Cypriot majority might attempt to do which in their view would threaten the security of their community. On the other hand the Greek Cypriots, because of their overwhelming majority, considered themselves to have the right to direct the affairs of Cyprus and were unsympathetic to the idea that the Turkish Cypriots should have anything but a modest say in the government. They chafed under the constitutional provisions that allowed certain bills coming before the 45-strong House of Representatives to be defeated, despite an overall majority vote in favour, if more than half the 15 Turkish Cypriot members voted against the bill. There were a number of other controversial clauses in the constitution over which there was never agreement. As the constitution became more and more unworkable, so the tensions rose and the relations between the two communities deteriorated until they broke down altogether and violence took over. As much as anything else, the question of municipality control brought about the final breach. The Greeks considered that separate municipal administration was unworkable, uneconomic and wasteful, whilst the Turks saw in an integrated but proportionately representative control a direct threat to those safeguards that they considered vital to their very existence. Neither side would compromise and when President Makarios put forward a 13-point formula for amending the constitution, it contained two proposals particularly unpalatable to the Turks: (1) abolition of the personal power of veto of the President and Vice-President (Turkish Cypriot, Dr Fazil Kutchuk), and (2) abolition of separate majorities for the enactment of certain laws in the House of Representatives. Under the constitution the power of veto could be exercised in respect of foreign affairs, defence and internal security. Had calm and rational consideration been given to the need for revising certain parts of the constitution subsequent events might have taken a different course, but there was nothing rational nor logical about the feelings existing at that time between the two communities; not even between the President and Vice-President was there any longer a bond of understanding or co-operation. Clandestine preparations for conflict had already begun and underground 'armies' were being equipped and re-trained for the day, now not far distant, when they would be required. On the Greek side the EOKA organization had never been fully disbanded and now formed the nucleus of the new fighter groups that were being raised. The Turks had no previous organization upon which to build, but soon established one with help from motherland Turkey.

On 21 December, 1963, the first clash occurred, in which two Turkish Cypriots were shot dead and another Turk and a Greek wounded. From then on, up to and including Christmas, the fighting became widespread and heavy throughout the capital, Nicosia, where the Turks had barricaded themselves in their own quarter and manned the entry points. How many people died during this period will probably never be known. Fighter groups of both sides roamed the streets in an orgy of genocide.* Both the Greek and Turkish Cypriot authorities had temporarily lost control of their own forces, the latter being out of touch with the situation in their suburban areas where some of the worse acts of murder and plunder were committed. Attempts by the two leaders to bring the fighting to a halt failed, the gunmen ignored their calls to stop.

The fighting could have gone on unchecked but for the intervention of the United Kingdom along with her fellow guarantors, Greece and Turkey. By treaty, Britain had retained her

---

* In June, 1964, the former EOKA leader General Grivas returned to Cyprus and took charge of the direction of the Greek Cypriot Military Operations. His first step was to reorganize the Fighter Groups into one disciplined body, later to be known as the Greek Cypriot National Guard. Thereafter, only the Turkish Fighter Groups were normally referred to as The Fighters.

sovereign bases in Cyprus after independence and occupied two areas on the south coast around Dhekelia and Episkopi. Also by treaty Greece and Turkey were permitted to maintain military contingents on the island—that of Greece 950 strong, that of Turkey 650. The three countries now offered to join together in providing a peace force to supervise a cease-fire and assist the Cyprus Government in the maintenance of law and order. This offer was accepted by the leaders of both communities.*
On 26 December, British troops, under the command of Major-General Peter Young, the commander of the Near East Land Forces in the sovereign bases, moved into the Republic to join the Greek and Turkish national contingents in a peacekeeping role. In the event, it was the British troops who bore the full brunt of this responsibility, for almost as soon as the fighting broke out both of the other contingents left their neutral camps and joined their Cypriot brothers in the field. The Turkish contingent never returned to its camp but remained inside the Turkish Cypriot enclave which now extended from Nicosia to the town of Kyrenia on the north coast; and although the Greek contingent did return to its camp, General Young, who had been designated the overall commander of the tripartite peace force, was never confident about using them except in liaison duties.

General Young's most pressing and immediate task was to bring about a permanent cease-fire in Nicosia. An uncertain truce was being maintained and could not be expected to last for long. Some kind of *cordon sanitaire* was needed into which neither side would be permitted to step and over which the British troops would have complete control. Eventually Young had his way and the 'green line' came into existence. But what

---

* By now, all Turkish Cypriots in Government Departments and the House of Representatives, including ministers and senior civil servants, had ceased to perform their duties, but had established their own administration within their quarter of the city.

was intended as a temporary expedient became a permanent 'frontier' and in the long run was to prove an 'unremitting obstacle to progress towards normalization between the two communities'.*

The British force remained in the Republic for three months before being relieved by a United Nations peacekeeping force. During that time, the conflict spread from Nicosia to every corner of the island. For the British troops it was a thankless task, for there was still considerable prejudice and antagonism in some quarters against them being stationed in the Republic; it was a little too soon after the EOKA days for comfort. This open antipathy, played up in the press, did nothing to make the job of peacekeeping easier and it was clear that it would be advisable, sooner rather than later, for them to be replaced by an international force of some kind. At a conference in London in February 1964, at which President Makarios and representatives of the Guarantor Powers were present, it was agreed to ask for a United Nations peace force to be established in Cyprus as soon as possible. On 4 March, 1964, the Security Council adopted a resolution to that effect and the first elements of UNFICYP began arriving in the island a few weeks later.

3

The United Nations Force in Cyprus (UNFICYP) was fully operational by the end of June 1964, by which time the strength of Britain's military participation had decreased to nearly half its original 3,000 men. The Government of Cyprus had accepted a British contingent as part of the Force, a break from the previous understanding that permanent member countries of the Security Council would not provide contingents for UN

* *The Impartial Soldier* by M. Harbottle.

peacekeeping forces, and along with contingents from Austria, Canada, Denmark, Finland, Ireland and Sweden, the United Kingdom has been a part of UNFICYP ever since—and a substantial part of it at that. For most of its existence the contingent numbered around 1,400, a quarter of UNFICYP's total strength. In addition to an infantry battalion, an armoured-car squadron and a helicopter flight, it includes a transport squadron and detachments of the other administrative services, as well as staff representation at the Force headquarters. As an additional contribution to the operation, the United Kingdom made available the facilities of the military administrative base at Dhekelia which throughout has provided the logistic backing for the whole Force, a total contribution in practical and material terms of £1,000,000 a year. The advantages of such a ready-made logistic support base can be well appreciated when compared to what was available in Egypt and the Congo. The two well-equipped military and RAF hospitals at Dhekelia and Akrotiri provide an impressive medical back-up to the small field hospital operated by the Austrian contingent. For all these reasons, the senior logistic officer at Force Headquarters has always been a British Lieutenant-Colonel and the chief medical officer a British Colonel. The appointment of Chief of Staff and Deputy Force Commander was also held by the British contingent commander, a Brigadier, until August 1968, when the Canadian contingent commander took over.

Along with the military there exists a small civilian police component, 170 strong and comprising Australians, Austrians, Danes, New Zealanders* and Swedes. Although civilian police had previously been used in the Congo, where first Ghanaian and then Nigerian policemen carried out normal routine police duties, and in West Irian where police officers from a number of countries replaced the departing Dutch and took over the running of the existing Papuan police force, Cyprus was the first

* Withdrawn in June 1968.

operation in which an element of this kind had been included. UNCIVPOL* has proved a decided success. Its duties are not those of a normal police force. It has no powers of arrest or detention, search or interrogation, nor any kind of executive authority. In all respects it is impartial, acting as an effective team of investigators, observers, negotiators, mediators, reporters—and father confessors. It mans police posts in sensitive areas, provides liaison officers at certain Greek and Turkish Cypriot police stations, carries out street, urban and rural patrols and helps to supervise the harvesting and cultivation of crops by one community in areas adjacent to or under the control of the other. The performance of this unique band of international policemen did much to assist in reducing the tension and establishing a calmer atmosphere. In contrast to a soldier, a policeman is often better suited to deal with situations that arise when matters of civil law and civic rights are concerned. In Cyprus UNCIVPOL has certainly gained a highly respected reputation which it thoroughly deserves.

Controlling and directing the peacekeeping operation is a headquarters of truly multi-national content. Apart from the military and the police, there is a civilian secretariat composed of representatives from twenty-five different countries—men and women from a wide variety of social and ideological backgrounds. The job of the Secretariat is to co-ordinate, supervise and deal with the financial, administrative and legal aspects of the operation as well as meeting its day-to-day requirements in materials and manpower. In this respect its head, the Chief Administrative Officers, leans heavily on the military Chief Logistics Officer for advice. As an off-shoot from the main secretariat, there is a small political department which is immediately answerable to the Special Representative of the UN Secretary-General. He is the civilian head of UNFICYP. He and the Force Commander work in parallel and are closely

* United Nations Civilian Police.

interlinked,* while their two respective senior staff members, the Senior Legal and Political Adviser and the Chief of Staff, act in unison and on joint matters of policy as a two-man secretariat to them. Both the Force Commander (who is responsible for the overall conduct of the peacekeeping operation) and the Special Representative (who is responsible for furthering UN efforts towards a peaceful solution in the political field) have direct access to the Secretary-General; though in normal circumstances they report and advise jointly on the developing situation.

It is this harmony and close working relationship at the top that has done so much to strengthen the authority of UNFICYP and make it the success that it has been. With this element of collaboration and co-operation permeating throughout the Force, the misunderstandings and frictions, which can so easily affect the unity of a force of this kind, have not materialized and UNFICYP has remained a remarkably happy establishment. It goes without saying, that such a relationship among a mixed force of civilians and soldiers naturally improves the performance of that force in effectiveness and efficiency.

4

A chronology of dates and actions, even to students of history, can prove very indigestible. In dealing with the UNFICYP operation my intention is to highlight particular milestones and events in the course of its history, to illustrate some of its successes and failures, and to present a cross-section of the kind of roles it has been called upon to play—roles which are not necessarily particular to Cyprus but are ones that could be met with in other and future peacekeeping operations.

* In UNEF there was only a Force Commander and there was a Civilian Chief of Operations in the Congo, to whom the military commander was subordinate.

Because of its size Cyprus posed no deployment problem. It was possible to divide the island into six areas of responsibility, one for each contingent. The original dispositions, with only one exception, remained the same until 1970, though from time to time there was some adjustment of the boundaries between contingents. Areas generally corresponded with the island's administrative district boundaries. The Danes and Finns were in Nicosia, the Canadians in the north around Kyrenia, the Irish in the north-west, the British in the south and the Swedes in the east.

The Danes and Finns kept the peace along the Green Line where the two communities were separated by the width of a narrow bazaar street, and where a thrown brick, a shout of abuse or the accidental discharge of a rifle could start a gun fight of major proportions. This was a task of observation and patrolling with the degree of observation measured in tens rather than hundreds of yards, a gruelling test of alertness and vigilance for any soldier; but these conscripted men from Scandinavia fulfilled their duties very well and never allowed an incident to develop into a prolonged shooting match.

The Canadians and Irish had similar responsibilities along the lower slopes of the Kyrenia and Troodos ranges respectively. Here the armed forces of the two communities had dug themselves in and confronted each other across a hundred yards or more of no-man's land. It was within this narrow strip of ground that the Canadians and Irish patrolled and manned O.Ps. It was no easier than it was for the Danes and Finns to prevent an interchange of shooting; all that was possible was to bring it to a halt as quickly as possible after it had started and ensure that it did not escalate into something worse. Although there was much shooting in these two areas over the years, neither side ever attacked the other, nor did the shooting get beyond the powers of the two contingents to contain. This was no mean achievement since they were dealing with young trigger-happy

10. *General K. S. Thimayya, UNFICYP Commander, with General Grivas and Archbishop Makarios. Famagusta, February, 1965.*

11. *Ferret Scout cars of A Squadron 5th Royal Inniskilling Dragoon Guards on patrol in southern Cyprus.*

12. The heads of UNFICYP, February, 1968. Left to right—Dr Remy Gorg̱ (Switzerland), Senior Legal and Political Adviser; Señor Bibiano Osorio-Tafa (Mexico), Secretary-General's Special Representative; Lt-General Arme Martola (Finland), Force Commander; Brigadier Michael Harbottle (UK Chief-of-Staff.

13. The author briefing Mr Denis Healey, then Minister of Defence, at Ayic Theodhoros, May, 1968.

soldiers of the National Guard and even younger Turkish Cypriot irregular fighters, who in the dark mistook every bush for an enemy soldier and every goat for a fighting patrol; it was no wonder that the shooting was frequent and prolonged.

For the Swedish and United Kingdom contingents it was different. Although in real estate they shared two-thirds of the island, from Polis in the north-west right round to Cape Andreas in the north-east, they could operate in a more flexible and mobile fashion. Except at Larnaca (Swedish zone) and for a while at Kophinou (British zone) there were no lines of confrontation as in the other zones. The operations were therefore much more fluid and spontaneous, needing quick reaction and counter-action by the UN to interpose a presence before a minor local incident could develop into an island-wide one. Escalation was likely to be both sudden and rapid, as was illustrated by the occasion when a group of Turkish fighters stopped and held a busload of Greek Cypriots for half an hour. Inside two hours a National Guard battalion with sixteen armoured cars was on its way from Nicosia to deal with the situation. This example of the volatile and excessive reactions of both sides to the smallest incident helps to illustrate the unceasing watchfulness and preparedness necessary on the part of every UN soldier to ensure that the UN reacted with sufficient speed to interpose itself between the two contestants.

5

The Cyprus operation is a play in three acts with countless scenes. The first act, or prologue, leading up to the UN intervention, has already been described. Act 2, the longest so far, covers the period from 1964 to 1968 with its emphasis on military operations, and Act 3, in which political and diplomatic manoeuvre has taken over from military action, is still in progress—the curtain has not yet fallen; whether or not the play will have a happy ending remains undecided. For three years the dialogue to find a peaceful settlement has been continuing. No real measure of agreement has been reached, but the talks still go on in the hope that an acceptable formula will be found. In the meantime UNFICYP continues to stand guard. The serious shooting ceased more than three years ago. Since then the island has remained relatively quiet. During the second six months of 1970 there were only 11 shooting incidents, as compared with nearly 400 in the comparable period of 1967. But the UNFICYP presence remains necessary so long as armed confrontation exists between Greek and Turk. Once that is removed and the National Guard withdrawn to its barracks and relegated to a reserve liability, the Turkish Cypriot fighters would melt away and turn their attention to a more worthwhile and productive existence. The day that motherland Turkey stops paying the fighter a monthly wage two to three times greater than he would otherwise be earning, just to encourage him to stay in the trenches, the fighter groups will disband. No one can live at peace in Cyprus so long as the armed confrontation prevails.

The story of those four years from March 1964, onwards, can best be described in a series of cameos—set against a backcloth of constant turbulence and strife, where the areas of tension and potential strife increased rather than decreased. Against this background the tasks and achievements of UNFICYP can better be appreciated.

In August 1964, UNFICYP faced its first serious threat to the success of its mission. There had been continuing widespread clashes between the two communities since the beginning in Larnaca, Limassol and Paphos, where in March the municipal market had been burnt to the ground and eleven civilians killed by Turkish Cypriot fighters. In Nicosia the uncertain truce prevailed, though the situation was far from stable and the periodic outbreaks of indiscriminate shooting did nothing to reduce tension. The Kyrenia hills had also been the scene of some serious fighting, around the periphery of the self-established Turkish Cypriot enclave which lay astride the Nicosia-Kyrenia road, barring its use to all Greek Cypriot traffic. This was the largest of three Turkish Cypriot enclaves, the other two being on the north-west coast at Kokkina and Limnitis in Lefka District—and the responsibility of the Swedish contingent.* It was the Kokkina bridgehead that was the scene of UNFICYP's first major crisis.

During the summer of 1964 there had been reports of an extensive arms smuggling operation across the beaches at Kokkina and Mansoura, two neighbouring villages with small fishing harbours. The arms brought in by small boats, allegedly from Turkey, were then being distributed throughout the Turkish village fighter groups around the island. It was also suspected that Turkey was using these smuggling trips to infiltrate large numbers of Turkish Cypriot youths, who had been given military training in Turkey, as well as introducing Turkish Army officers into the island to command and train the fighter groups. The Cyprus Government warned UNFICYP that unless it put a stop to this activity, the Government would have to take action of its own. UNFICYP could not forcibly intervene to prevent the alleged arms smuggling since it did not have the mandate to do so (a weakness in the mandate that might have been solved had there been a UN coastal patrol force working in conjunction with UNFICYP. Throughout there was clandestine smuggling of men and weapons by both sides). UNFICYP could only exhort both sides to refrain from any action that might disturb the peace, while in New York UN diplomatic efforts were being directed at urging Turkey to stop the despatch of arms to Cyprus. The Cyprus Government assured the Force Commander that it had no immediate intention of taking military

* Later the Swedes exchanged places with the Irish in Famagusta.

action and that were it to do so it would give due and timely warning. This assurance had been asked for and given after a National Guard force, 2,000 strong, had been moved into positions around the two villages.

So the sword of Damocles hung poised, while UNFICYP redoubled its efforts to secure the guarantees that the Government was insisting upon. Unfortunately it was not to be allowed the time in which to achieve a solution. On 3 August a patrol boat of the Greek Cypriot navy* was fired on from the shore when passing close in to Mansoura. It returned the fire before withdrawing out of range. Two days later firing broke out again, this time between the opposing land forces and continued until the 10th when UNIFCYP's commander, General Thimayya of India, procured a cease-fire. On the 6th the Government forces launched a ground attack on the Kokkina bridgehead. In the heavy fighting that followed both sides suffered casualties, though not as many as might have been expected,† but the Turkish forward positions were driven in and the size of the bridgehead greatly diminished.

The attack and the firing that preceded it had come without warning; no notice had been given by the Government as promised. As a result, the UN soldiers were caught in the middle and it was considered necessary to withdraw them from their positions until fighting stopped. This was not done solely to ensure the safety of the Swedes; since the battle was fully joined, there was nothing they could do to influence events until a cease-fire or a disengagement occurred. Once this happened the Swedes immediately re-interposed themselves between the two sides, but their absence had meant that there was no restraining influence while they were away. As will be seen in a later incident, the continued presence of UN soldiers on the

* A flotilla of five torpedo boats.
† A feature of most of the fighting that took place was maximal expenditure of ammunition for minimal casualties.

battlefield did serve a useful purpose and helped to shorten the fighting.

At one point in the fighting the Turkish Air Force intervened with fighter and light-bomber support for their beleagured Turkish Cypriot comrades. They flew a series of sorties, strafing and bombing the National Guard positions surrounding Kokkina and also civilian traffic moving along the road running eastwards from the bridgehead. This was a direct violation of Cyprus air space, but having no means of retaliation the Government was forced to grin and bear it—not for the only time either.

The problems of the aftermath lasted longer than the battle itself. The plight of the Turkish villages was serious and UNFICYP initially experienced great difficulty in getting essential supplies and medical aid to them, owing to a Government order forbidding the movement of all forms of supply into Turkish-controlled areas. By patient and persuasive negotiation General Thimayya eventually overcame this obstacle, and though the island-wide embargo was to remain in force until 1967, the restriction was temporarily lifted to allow a mercy mission into the Kokkina bridgehead. The food supplies and hygienic facilities within the bridgehead were quite inadequate to cope with the heavy influx of refugees from outlying areas taken over by the National Guard, especially after the heavy shelling and mortaring that Kokkina and Mansoura had received. Even then it was not until mid-September that the first supply convoys got through. In spite of its failure in this first round to prevent a renewal of the fighting, UNFICYP played a significant part in containing it and succouring the victims.

General Grivas, the former EOKA leader who had returned to Cyprus to form and take command of the National Guard, seemed to delight in taking unilateral initiatives which invariably resulted in a rise in tension and more problems for UNFICYP. He was contemptuous of the Turkish Cypriots and believed that the only thing they responded to was force. He was forever 'sabre-rattling' and sometimes withdrew the blade from its scabbard.

Mora and Melousha, two Turkish Cypriot villages lying to the east of Nicosia, were the scene of two attempts by Grivas to 'teach the Turks a lesson'. In the instance of Mora it was reported to him that the Turks were building trenches on the south side of the village where it overlooked the old Nicosia-Famagusta road. Without waiting for UNFICYP to investigate and take appropriate action, Grivas sent a mixed force of military and police, around a hundred in strength and supported by armoured cars, to deal with the problem. Luckily the Finnish contingent commander, Colonel Uolevi Koskenpalo, in whose area Mora was situated, was alerted to the situation and went at once to the village, where he discovered the Turks refurbishing existing trenches, but not digging new ones. Though tactless and provocative, it was not the serious matter that Grivas claimed it to be. Koskenpalo deployed a company of his Finns between the village and the road where Grivas' men were now halted. Grivas and his second-in-command, Prokos, both generals, were there, personally directing their hundred-strong force. Koskenpalo persuaded the Turks to stop working on their trenches, while he went to talk to Grivas. Grivas was not an easy man to deal with at such moments, but Uolevi Koskenpalo was a tall, squarely-built man who towered above the diminutive general. When the latter started shouting that he was going to deal with the Turks once and for all, Koskenpalo told him very sharply, 'Stop shouting, General, I am a Finnish Colonel and I will not be shouted at'; and that was the end of the matter. Grivas left the scene; Koskenpalo succeeded in persuading Prokos to withdraw his force in return for the abandonment and filling in of the Turkish trenches and, that settled, everyone went home.

The Melousha incident was not so easily resolved, though its conclusion was every bit as successful. The Mora contretemps had taken place on the morning of 23 July. Even as it was being peacefully resolved, Grivas was reacting to a situation that had developed at nearby Melousha. Early in the afternoon of the same day, a Cyprus police landrover had driven through this Turkish Cypriot village, its occupants brandishing their weapons and shouting abuse, a totally unnecessary and provocative act, particularly since the villagers were on friendly terms with their two neighbouring Greek Cypriot villages. To add to the provocation, the police, who could well have been returning to Larnaca from the incident at Mora, set up a roadblock on the far side of the village. This brought a reaction from the local fighter group, who took up positions and prevented the police patrol from returning through the village when they attempted to do so.

One wonders whether this adventure was pre-planned, for all Grivas did when he received the news was to switch his Mora force to Melousha with instructions that it was to disarm every Turk in the place. This posed an even greater threat than Mora because there was no doubt that Grivas, having already been thwarted in his designs once that day, was determined not to frustrated again. At the time there was only a platoon of Swedes in the area and they were quickly interposed between the village and the direction from which the National Guard was advancing. The time was about 1630.

There followed nine hours of negotiation between the Swedish contingent commander, Colonel Lars Lavén, who had come to the spot immediately, and the National Guard commander whose force was now halted in the next village a few miles down the road from Melousha. Each time Lavén reported that negotiations had broken down he was urged to keep on trying. Meanwhile, as he continued to talk, the UN force was being strengthened behind him. Another Swedish platoon was on the move from Famagusta, a Danish and a Finnish platoon were also on their way, while two troops of the 8th Canadian Hussars were coming from Nicosia* and were to be joined later by two detachments of 105mm anti-tank guns from their compatriots, the 1st Bn The Black Watch of Canada, at Kyrenia.

Around 0200 a dispirited Lavén reported that he had exhausted all possibilities and there was nothing more he could do. Force Headquarters had been unable until then to contact Grivas, nor had approaches to the Ministry of Interior proved any more successful. It was imperative to keep negotiations going for a little longer, until the UN task force had assembled at Melousha. At 0300 Grivas was contacted at his house at the National Guard barracks. The Chief of Staff† met him there on the instructions of the Force Commander (now General Armas Martola of Finland) and warned him that if his troops attacked Melousha UNFICYP would use force to stop them; since the UN was now interposed, the National Guard would have to attack through the UN positions, and were they to do so the UN troops had a right to act in self-defence. The meeting with Grivas lasted until daybreak, by which time the sun and the game were up: for UNFICYP'S deployments were now complete and the UN task force was superior in men and weapons. There was nothing for Grivas to do but to withdraw. By the evening of 24 July all troops were back in their respective camps.

Arsos was a neighbour of Melousha but one of the few totally integrated villages in Cyprus, where Greeks and Turks enjoyed a friendly existence side by side in next-door houses. But in September 1966, two murders followed each other in quick succession, first a Turk, then a Greek. It is likely that the cause

---

* These two troops under the command of their squadron leader, Major Art St Aubin, drove straight through the advancing National Guard in order to reach Melousha before them, and were waved on by the military police on traffic duty.

† The author.

of the first was a private feud and that the second was a reprisal for the first, but in the existing political temperature the outcome was predictable. The second killing was followed by a a whole fusillade of shots from windows and from doorways, criss-crossing the village. This indescriminate shooting would have continued unabated and certainly innocent women and children would have been killed had not a resourceful Swedish platoon commander ordered his men into the houses where the shooting was coming from, to disarm the fighters. Since the UN soldiers had no mandate to disarm them forcibly, they could but persuade the fighters to lay down their weapons voluntarily. This they succeeded in doing—a remarkably cool and courageous performance. Although the fighters regained their weapons later and the village remained a disturbed place for a long time, the prompt action of the UN had the effect of stopping the fighting.

Sometimes there was an amusing side to these incidents. Once, at Mari, a Turkish village on an escarpment overlooking the Nicosia-Limassol road just south of Kophinou, a serious situation developed when a National Guard armoured-car patrol opened fire on the Turkish fighter positions commanding the road. At one point the warrant officer in command lost complete control of himself and poured round after round into a civilian car, parked empty on the side of the road only a few feet away from his gun muzzle. In his frenzy the warrant officer must have cost the taxpayer close to £100 in expended ammunition—a truly expensive way of giving vent to one's feelings!

In all, well over a thousand rounds of small arms and forty two-pounder shells were fired during the engagement, causing the death of a donkey and a goat two miles away. The owner of the donkey, an old woman, was wounded in the leg—she was compensated later by the Government. Because of the height of the escarpment and the angle of elevation on the guns of the armoured cars, it was not surprising that there were plenty of 'overs', but only one other casualty was reported. This was in the camp of 'A' Squadron of the Royal Inniskilling Dragoon Guards (UNFICYP's second armoured-car squadron) at Zyyi, which lay in direct line of fire three miles behind the escarpment. One of the two-pounder shells landed on the road in front of the ration store, bounced through the open doorway and into a basket of eggs, breaking two of them.

UNFICYP's peacekeeping efforts were not only confined to military actions of the kind so far described. UNFICYP had many facets and not least of these was the joint civilian-military collaboration in easing the domestic difficulties arising out of the economic blockade, which imposed great hardship on the Turkish Cypriots. UNFICYP's legal and political department concentrated on achieving the relaxation of the economic restrictions and the restoration of freedom of movement. At the same time the military and UNCIVPOL did what they could to ensure that both communities were able to till their fields, harvest their crops, graze their flocks, educate their children and undertake as many of the normal activities of life as possible, particularly in areas of armed confrontation and mixed villages: areas in which it was easier for the military rather than civilians to operate. A special staff branch* at Force Headquarters existed to co-ordinate these activities—a military staff with no specialist qualities, acting through the contingents and co-ordinating its field work with UNFICYP's political department. Besides its supervisory duties, the branch dealt with disputes over land and water rights as they occurred, undertook the distribution of vital economic and medical supplies, mail, and even examination papers to Turkish centres in areas outside Nicosia. It assisted in the movement of doctors, nurses, school-teachers and the sick to and from the bridgeheads of Kokkina and Limnitis. In these and many other ways the branch did a remarkable job and made an enormous contribution to the quietening of tension

* Operations (Economics).

and the restoration of confidence among the people of both communities.

In the British-supervised district of Paphos in July and August 1967, a series of murders and disappearances totally disrupted the lives of its inhabitants. Over a period of four weeks, 6 Greeks and 5 Turks were murdered and at least another 6 Turks disappeared, never to re-appear. The effect on both communities was considerable. No one would venture outside the limits of their village for fear of being the next victim. Fields and vineyards, even those immediately adjacent to the villages, went untended. Greek and Turk went in terror of their lives and the whole economic life of the region came to a halt. Doctors had to be escorted on their rounds by the UN. Food from Paphos was delivered to outlying villages in supply convoys organized and escorted by UN armoured cars. No amount of persuasion could get the situation back to normal. However, the inhabitants of every village visited by an UNFICYP investigation team stressed that they had no militant tendencies towards their neighbours; all they wanted, they said, was to be allowed to live and work in peace. This common theme prompted the idea for a series of meetings between the mukhtars* of neighbouring Greek and Turkish villages at which each could assure the other, face to face, that there was no threat of violence from his village nor any ban on freedom of movement through it. With the co-operation of the Government and Turkish Cypriot Leadership 16 meetings were arranged of which only 2 failed to take place; at some as many as 8 villages were represented. An UNFICYP officer was present at each meeting in the capacity of referee†. The initiative paid off. Not only did the economic life of the area begin again but a new co-operation developed from this renewal, after nearly four years,

* Village headmen.

† The Duke of Wellington's Regiment was at the time responsible for Paphos District and provided the officers.

of personal contact between the villages of the two communities. Quiet diplomacy and simple reasoning succeeded where tougher tactics might have failed.

During the late summer and early autumn of 1967 a situation developed which nearly put paid to the United Nations peace effort in Cyprus—and all because of one policeman and his beat. For two and a-half years Sergeant 'John' from Skarinou had cycled regularly each week one mile down the road to the mixed village of Ayios Theodhoros; the fact that he had to pass through the Turkish end of the village before reaching the Greek quarter had never posed any difficulty as he was well known from the day when Ayios Theodhoros had a police station of its own—that is until the Turkish fighters came and disturbed the comparative calm of the place. After two serious outbreaks of shooting during July the Cyprus police temporarily suspended the weekly visits; but when in September it was decided to restart them, the Turkish fighters barred the way and forced the sergeant and his escort to use an alternative route, a goat track, which avoided the Turkish part of the village.

From this small beginning, there developed a political situation which escalated as high as the corridors of the United Nations Headquarters and brought Greece and Turkey to the brink of war. The wrangle lasted until mid-November, by which time Greece, Turkey and the Secretary-General were fully involved in the controversy. The Turkish Cypriot Leadership attempted to make the settlement of the issue conditional upon the removal of the Government's blockade elsewhere in the island—a condition which the Government would not agree to, nor the UN support. The Government demanded the restitution of freedom of movement for the patrol, with no strings attached; it did, however, accede to UNIFICYP's urgings not to take enforcement action to implement its demand, but to allow UNFICYP to negotiate a settlement with the Turks.

It is tragic that the Government's patience ran out just as the UN had nearly reached a settlement. On 14 November, despite UNIFICYP's disclosure that a settlement was in sight and that confirmation was expected very shortly that Turkey had accepted the *status quo ante*, a police patrol escorted by armoured cars and infantry from the National Guard force at Skarinou, drove into the Turkish end of Ayios Theodhoros and through it to the Greek quarter, returning by the same road half an hour later. There was no reaction from the Turkish villagers and the fighters were conspicuous by their absence. In most people's view the Government had made their point and no further gesture was necessary, but they reckoned without General Grivas. The general not only followed the morning sorties with an afternoon visit of his own, but he mounted another strongly escorted patrol the next morning. There seems little doubt that he was determined to provoke the Turks into a fight, for even while UNFICYP's Force Commander, General Martola, and Señor Osorio Tafall, U Thant's Special Representative, were making strong representations to the Cyprus Government to stop this provocative action, Grivas ordered yet another patrol into the village in the early afternoon of the 15th. For him, it had the desired effect—a shot was fired as the patrol reached the village. Whether it came from a National Guard or fighter's rifle is not known, but it was the prologue to a battle that lasted for ten hours, during which machine guns, mortars and field artillery were used against the village and its close neighbour Kophinou, in which the fighter base for that area was located. Before the shooting had finished, 22 Turks had been killed, many of them civilians lying in the ruins of their homes, and 9 more had been wounded. During the whole of the engagement the UN OP's around the two villages remained manned despite the fact that they were in direct line of fire throughout. From them came a non-stop commentary of what was happening and it was largely due to these soldiers of the Royal Green Jacket

Regiment that UNFICYP was able to procure as early a cease-fire as it did, and later to scotch exaggerated reports of atrocities. This is no idle claim, for as these eye-witness reports came in it became horrifyingly clear to everyone, the Cyprus and Greek Governments included, how far Grivas had gone, thus strengthening UNFICYP's hand in demanding a halt to the action.

The consequences of 15 November were internationally serious and far-reaching. Turkey threatened intervention and massed a seaborne force at Iskenderun, 150 miles from Famagusta and its ideal invasion beaches. Her aircraft repeatedly flew over the island in the weeks that followed, quite unchallenged. War between Greece and Turkey appeared inevitable and was expected daily but was averted in the end due to the exhaustive efforts of José Rolz Bennett,* whom U Thant sent as his personal representative to the three governments concerned to mediate a settlement, and Mr Cyrus Vance, who acted in the same capacity for President Johnson. These two men spared no efforts in their attempts to avert war—and succeeded.

The 15 November, 1967, will be remembered in Cyprus as a turning point in its affairs. From that moment on there has been no more fighting. The Greek National Army units that had been clandestinely brought to the island over the previous four years were withdrawn in January 1968, although Greek army officers remained with the National Guard. Grivas did not last a week after his débâcle at Ayios Theodhoros—he was recalled to Athens on 19 November and has remained there in suspended military animation ever since.

In his turn President Makarios removed all economic embargoes and movement restrictions on the Turkish Cypriot community in December 1967, and tension decreased appreciably. But regretfully it was not to be the beginning of the end,

* One of the then two Under-Secretaries-General for Political Affairs. Dr Ralph Bunche was the other.

but rather the beginning of the stalemate, which continues to this day.

Why was it that UNFICYP did not step in and interpose itself at Ayios Theodhoros, as it had at Melousha, and threaten to use force to prevent the attack if it was made? Whereas Grivas' planned attack on Melousha had not been provoked, other than by his own police, at Ayios Theodhoros the Turkish Cypriots were wholly responsible for the situation developing as it did. The UN supported the Cyprus Government's demand for the restoration of freedom of movement to the village; it could not therefore protect the Turkish Cypriots against what it considered to be the legal right of the Greeks. By escorting the police patrol, Grivas was doing no more than UNFICYP had once done in the early days of the controversy—even though UNFICYP deplored the decision of the Government to go ahead with the patrolling against its advice. In retrospect, it is possible to think of ways in which an intervention might have been made in the very first moments of battle,* but for UNFICYP to have acted against the patrol at any time prior to the opening of fire would have been supporting the guilty party.

A postscript to this near-calamitous incident is worth telling. In December 1967 when invasion threatened and war between Greece and Turkey seemed imminent, the Greek and Turkish Cypriots at Ayios Theodhoros were once again sitting together in their coffee shops, not only exchanging conversation but also exchanging Christmas presents.

6

The UNFICYP story is not complete without proper mention being made of its untiring efforts in the political field to bring about a *rapprochement* between the two communities; an effort

* See *The Impartial Soldier.*

which was made more difficult by the often uncomprehending attitudes of the two mother countries, Greece and Turkey. In March 1964, the Secretary-General appointed Hr Sakari Tuomioja of Finland as Mediator in Cyprus, but in September he suffered a heart attack and died in Helsinki a few days later— hardly having begun his important task. In his place U Thant appointed Señor Galo Plaza, formerly President of Ecuador,* who for a time had been his Special Representative in Cyprus. Galo Plaza worked hard to find a basis on which a settlement might be founded. After six months during which he visited every part of the island and talked with many people from the highest to lowest, he presented a report of his findings. In it he made four main points: that Cyprus should remain an independent state, renouncing voluntarily its rights to choose union with Greece (ENOSIS); that the island should be demilitarized; that there should be no partition or physical separation of Greek and Turkish communities; and finally that any settlement must depend in the first place on the agreement between the people of Cyprus themselves and that talks should take place between Greek and Turkish Cypriots. In putting forward these points, Galo Plaza was not making recommendations but rather observations on what he considered fundamental to the start of settlement talks. Initial reaction within Cyprus was not wholly unfavourable and had it been left to the leaders of both communities there might have been some positive and constructive progress made. But first Turkey and then Greece rejected the report. No doubt angered by the implied reproof that the settlement of the Cyprus question was none of her business, Turkey ignored the 'keep out' notice and called for direct talks between herself and Greece—a call to which the Greek Government

* He is one of Ecuador's richest landowners. The story is told that, during one particularly difficult and abortive meeting with President Makarios, Galo Plaza in a moment of frustration exclaimed, 'Your Beatitude, you must appreciate that I can fit your island ten times into my estates at home'.

4. *The author briefing Mr Ralph Bunche, Cyprus, July, 1966.*

5. *Kashmir, 1955. Major Altieri (Uruguay) patrols the cease-fire line.*

16. *UN observers at an Indian outpost, 13,000 feet above sea-level.*

17. The War in Korea. Men of the US 9th Infantry Regiment aid a wounde soldier, September, 1950.

18. Korean refugees, fleeing the Communists, struggle southward through th snow, forced to keep off the main roads to avoid hindering military traffic, Januar 1951.

responded. The 'talks', when they started, dragged on for eighteen months without reaching any conclusion and only served to delay any possible settlement. Having had his report so emphatically rejected, Galo Plaza could do little else but resign as Mediator—there was no further useful purpose that he could serve in that capacity.

Since no new initiative was immediately apparent and since President Makarios felt disinclined to pursue any fresh initiative on his own part whilst the dialogue between Athens and Ankara continued, there was little point in appointing a successor to Galo Plaza—in any case it is doubtful if a nomination would have been acceptable to the three parties concerned. From then on, there was a vacuum in mediation and, though U Thant's Special Representative with UNFICYP, first Carlos Bernardes of Brazil and later Bibiano Osorio-Tafall of Mexico, worked in every way possible to reduce the political tension and the economic hardships with varying degrees of success, no further mediation effort was thereafter mounted.

The Colonels' take-over in Greece and the events of November 1967, made a significant change—and brought to a halt the abortive dialogue of the two parent powers. The door was once more open for mediation by the UN. Osorio-Tafall did not waste the opportunity; he worked assiduously and perseveringly through the early months of 1968 to bring the representatives of the two communities to the conference table. On 4 June, Glafcos Clerides, leader of the House of Representatives, and Rauf Denktash of the Turkish Cypriot Leadership, flew to Beirut for a brief meeting and three weeks later, on 24 June, they met again at the Ledra Palace Hotel in Nicosia where Osorio-Tafall, the architect of the talks, briefly took the chair before leaving the two men to their discussions.

It is true that two and a-half years later these talks are continuing with no apparent sign of a breakthrough. The road is going to be long. Maybe it could be considerably shortened were there to be a disengagement and a disbandment of the military forces. It is probable that the way would be made easier by the elimination of certain vested interests—of those who stand to gain by the continuance of the conflict. What is certain is that the large majority of the people and particularly the younger generation, long for the end of the strife and a return to peaceful co-existence—a co-existence that is perfectly possible and practical, as is already being demonstrated in the mixed villages all over the island. Ayios Theodhoros only happened because of the actions of a militant few; its inhabitants wasted no time in restoring the friendly inter-communal relationship that had existed before the fighters and National Guard came—before Grivas came to disturb their peace. What is possible at Ayios Theodhoros is not so impossible elsewhere.

CHAPTER 5

West Irian
1962-1963

I

The United Nations intervention in West Irian, formerly West New Guinea (Papua), deserves a chapter to itself for two significant reasons; first, it is the only instance in its history that the United Nations has assumed responsibility for the administration of a territory, and second, it ended on the day that had been originally announced that it would—a distinction that no other UN operation can claim.

The dispute that necessitated the intervention derived from the long-drawn-out wrangle over sovereignty between the Netherlands and Indonesia following the end of the Second World War. This had partly resolved itself at The Hague in 1949 with the recognition by the Netherlands of Indonesia as an independent and sovereign state. But there remained the question of West New Guinea's future on which agreement had not been reached. It was left open for further negotiation on the understanding that the island's political status would be decided within one year. There was ambiguity over whether or not the Netherlands retained sovereign rights over the territory during the period. The Netherlands Government insisted that she did, until such a time that the people of West New Guinea could decide their future for themselves, but Indonesia claimed that by the Hague Declaration the Netherlands had merely been given the right to administer the territory during the interim period and not the authority to exercise sovereignty over it.

The argument continued far beyond the stipulated one year and was not resolved when Indonesia took the matter to the UN in 1954. The Indonesians were demanding the incorporation of New Guinea into Indonesia, but at no session of the General Assembly was there a two-thirds majority vote in favour, the minimum necessary for a resolution to be adopted. Not until 1961 was any breakthrough discernible. By then the Dutch were finding the continuance of their colonial responsibilities an increasing burden and were actively searching for the means by which they could shed them. Their search was helped in October 1961, by an Assembly resolution* calling for the taking of immediate steps towards granting independence to those Trust or non-Self-Governing Territories still without it. Using this resolution as a basis, the Netherlands proposed that it should hand over to the United Nations the responsibility for administering West New Guinea until such a time as the people declared their preference for the future—independence or union with Indonesia. Admirable as this proposal might seem, it did not appeal to the Indonesians, who saw in it an attempt to deprive Indonesia of her rightful territory. In Jakarta on 24 October, the Foreign Minister, Dr Subandrio, claimed that Indonesia reserved the right 'to liberate our brothers in West Irian', by force of arms if necessary. President Sukarno followed this in December with a rabble-rousing speech calling for the liberation of West Irian. 'Let us fly the red and white flag of Indonesia over Papua', he cried, and it was not long before he was trying to do so. In January 1962 a small Indonesian naval force of torpedo boats was intercepted off Fak-Fak on the west coast of the island by units of the Dutch East Indies fleet. In the engagement that followed, one of the torpedo boats was sunk and the remainder fled. On board the sunken boat, apart from 35 soldiers, there had been a quantity of arms including mortars and

* General Assembly Resolution 1514 (XV)—October 1961.

machine guns. Later it was announced by the Indonesians that their Deputy Chief of Naval Staff, Commander Soedarso, had been killed in the action. Between March and June a number of paratroop landings were made at widely separated points, but these attempts at infiltration proved unsuccessful and were mostly liquidated by Dutch marines, though a few of the invaders remained at large in the jungle.

In May 1962, Ellsworth Bunker, a former US ambassador to India and later to be involved in the Yemen, was used by U Thant as a mediator to work out a plan agreeable to both sides. In this he was successful and the 'Bunker Plan' became the blueprint for West Irian's future. By it the Dutch handed over the administration to the UN, the UN would then exercise authority over the territory for not less than one year with the assistance of non-Indonesian and non-Dutch administrators. After not more than two years the administration would be transferred to the Indonesians who, at a future date, would give the people of West Irian the chance to exercise their freedom of voting on their future. The cost of the UN administration effort would be shared equally between the Netherlands and Indonesia.

This plan found favour with both sides. The period of the UN administration was agreed to last until May 1963, and the year of the self-determination plebiscite was to be 1969. In August the agreement was signed, but since there had been a continuation of the naval and military activity it was thought desirable that a small UN peacekeeping force should also be sent to West Irian. This force was provided entirely by Pakistan; 1,000 strong it was commanded by Brigadier-General Said Ud Khan, later U Thant's Representative in Nigeria during her recent civil war. The Secretary-General sent his Military Adviser, Brigadier Indar Rikhye, to West Irian to observe the cease-fire, set up an observer team and plan the deployment of the Pakistanis against their arrival.

2

The concept of a caretaker administration was a wholly new one for the United Nations. In the event it proved very successful. From all over the world, professional men, industrialists, engineers, technicians, forestry experts, health advisers, were recruited to take over governmental departments and public utilities from the Dutch and run them during the interregnum. The judiciary posed a special problem which in the end was resolved by the Dutch judges staying on until the handover to Indonesia. On the security side there was a national police force and a militia—the Papuan Volunteer Corps. The rank and file of the police were Papuans but the officers had all been Dutch. A multi-national cadre under a British officer, was raised to fill the executive posts so that the force could continue to operate effectively. Senior UN secretariat officials were seconded to take over senior positions in the Administration and Señor José Rolz Bennett, former *Chef de Cabinet* to U Thant, was appointed UN Administrator. To complete the team, some 500 former Dutch officials voluntarily remained behind to help. With a fixed term to run, every opportunity was taken to train up suitable Papuans to fill junior posts after the UN had left. Also, to ensure that the hand-over to the Indonesians went smoothly when the time came, those Indonesians nominated to take over executive posts in the administration and public and governmental services were brought in early.

West Irian is one of the largest islands in the world, but apart from a narrow coastal belt it is almost entirely covered by jungle. Many Papuans had never seen the sea until the UN came; some had never seen a white man. There is the story of a Papuan on his first trip to the coast who was not surprisingly overawed by all he saw in the shop windows, but more than anything else it was the sea that fascinated him. When the time came to return to his jungle village, it was not a transistor radio, a wristwatch or even a pair of shoes that he took home, but a bottle filled with sea water.

The dense jungle made it difficult, after the treaty had been signed, to inform those Indonesian paratroops still at large that there was a cease-fire. To help, the Indonesian Ministry of Defence notified Rikhye of the dropping zones, but it was very soon apparent that many had mistaken their DZ and had dropped elsewhere. The only means of communication existing was through the civil link Radio Jakarta. Many of the paratroopers had gone into action carrying their transistors. Some never turned up, but a number did report in as a result of radio announcements—and later formed part of a four-square UN Force, the Pakistan contingent, the Indonesian paratroops, the Papuan Volunteer Corps and the civil police.

United Nations Temporary Executive Authority (UNTEA) existed for eight months transferring responsibility for the administration of West Irian to Indonesia on 1 May, 1963—the date originally agreed for the hand-over. Besides the UN Security Force (UNSF), twenty-one observer teams were posted in the main towns and districts to deter any attempt to breach the cease-fire and to help prepare the outlying communities for the changes ahead. Drawn from UNEF, ONUC and UNTSO, they came as always from a cross-section of the countries of the world.

In accordance with the treaty, the West Irians exercised their Act of Free Choice in a UN-supervised plebiscite in July and August 1969. The issue for them to decide was whether or not they would remain in Indonesia. Overwhelmingly they elected to remain.

It is doubtful if the United Nations has ever performed a more democratic act of administration. Certainly in terms of success it heads the order of merit in the list of UN's achievements in the sphere of peacekeeping. It was also a clear indication of how a multi-national team of experts (only 35 strong)

can exercise peaceful and constitutional authority for a prescribed period of time during an interregnum in the political
affairs of a small state. This is not to say that problems did not
arise in West Irian—they did, but in the main they were skilfully
handled. Not least among them was the question of the United
Nations 'national anthem'. Shortly before the arrival on an
official visit of the Head of State of a neighbouring country, the
bandmaster of the Pakistani contingent came into General Said
Ud Khan's office and asked what anthem he should play at the
official welcome at the airport. He was told that the United
Nations had not got one; but he insisted that protocol would
not be served unless the band played the anthem of the visitor's
country first and that of the host country second. Eventually
the General left it to the bandmaster, suggesting that he should
play something that the band knew well and with this the bandmaster had to be content. On the day everything went according
to plan. The plane arrived on time, the Head of State appeared
at the top of the gangway steps and his national anthem was
played—then with a roll of drums and with everyone standing
stiffly to attention and at the salute, the band broke into the
unmistakeable strains of Mikis Theodorakis' 'Never on Sunday'
. . . never in a lifetime of Sundays could the United Nations
have been accorded a less appropriate anthem.

CHAPTER 6

Military
Observer
Missions
1946-1971

I

The United Nations have deployed a considerable number of missions of one kind or another, from fact-finding to military observation and supervisory teams. Some have comprised a single Special Representative, others have involved as many as 500 military officer observers. Their objectives have been to investigate, supervise and report. From the information that they provide, the Secretary-General, the Security Council and the General Assembly are better able to assess the facts and to adjudge the true state of affairs existing in the 'infected' area. The missions become the eyes and ears of the United Nations and in particular of the Secretary-General, who is normally responsible for their operations. In the case of the large military observer missions the objectives are broader, for not only do they report incidents, breaches of cease-fire and violations of armistice lines, but they carry out on-the-spot negotiations with the purpose of confining the initial incident and preventing it from escalating into a major military situation. Not all missions have been successful, some have achieved little because of a lack of co-operation from governments and states involved in the particular dispute, others have suffered from lack of funds or problems of terrain which have seriously curtailed their capability. But there are those that have, and still continue to, carry out their responsibilities and tasks with an effectiveness which justifies their continued existence.

This chapter focuses on four of the better known of the military observer operations, Palestine, Kashmir (and the India-Pakistan dispute), Lebanon and Yemen. To cover the full gamut of all UN peace missions and peace initiatives would require a separate volume of its own, but the part played by the UN in the Balkans between 1946 and 1954, in Indonesia from 1947–1951, in Cambodia in 1963 and 1964 and in the Dominican Republic in 1965 deserves a place in the study of international relations and the peaceful settlement of international disputes.

2

Palestine 1948–71. (See map, p. 9.)

The United Nations Truce Supervisory Organization (UNTSO) has existed for twenty-three years. Its establishment in June 1948, followed Britain's withdrawal from Palestine and her relinquishment of the Mandate which she had exercised there since 1918. During the previous two years the British army had been involved in a major internal security operation against various militant Jewish underground organizations—the Haganah and terrorist groups like the notorious Stern Gang. The Jews were demanding a separate autonomous state within Israel—a demand which the Arab world would not accept. Unable to find a solution, the United Kingdom placed the Palestine problem before the General Assembly with a request that a special commission be set up to make recommendations for its future government. On 23 April the Security Council approved a resolution establishing a Truce Commission (UNSCOP) and a month later a Mediator was appointed—Count Bernadotte, a member of the Royal House of Sweden, head of the Swedish Red Cross and a much respected international diplomat. His primary task was to work for a peaceful adjustment of the Palestine problem and to use his good offices with the local authorities to bring about a more settled situation in Palestine.

There had been sporadic fighting inside Palestine and along its borders for some months before Bernadotte's arrival. When on 15 May the British Mandate came to an end, the Jews proclaimed the establishment of the State of Israel. The reaction of the Arab States was immediate. The armies of Egypt (Trans-Jordan, Syria, Iraq and Lebanon) advanced across their frontiers and heavy fighting followed on all fronts. The Security Council called for an immediate cease-fire and on 29 May succeeded in arranging a four-week truce; it was to be the first of many. In order to increase the effectiveness of its added responsibilities for supervising the cease-fire, the Truce Commission requested the assistance of military advisers and observers. The Security Council agreed but it was left to Bernadotte to recruit them. The initial observer group numbered 21 and came from those countries already forming the Truce Commission, Belgium, France and USA. It formed the basis on which UNTSO was later to be organized; for it was to change in character and mandate four times over the years. By September the number of observers had increased to 300, indicating the extent to which the situation had developed. Fighting had flared up again and although a second cease-fire was arranged on 15 July it was to be violated on a number of occasions. However, first Bernadotte and later Dr Ralph Bunche worked unceasingly to effect a more permanent truce. These efforts were tragically disrupted in September 1948, by the assassination of Count Bernadotte. Travelling with the Chief of Staff of UNTSO, General Lindstrom, Colonel Serot of France and two American officers on a tour of inspection, the Mediator's car was blocked by a jeep in a Jewish-held quarter of Jerusalem. Out of the jeep jumped two armed gunmen, one of whom fired into the car at point blank range killing Colonel Serot outright and fatally wounding Bernadotte, who died moments later. One of the Americans, Colonel Begley, was wounded as he wrestled with the second gunman. Later the Stern Gang claimed responsibility for the crime, stating that Bernadotte was killed because 'he worked for the British and carried out their orders'—the kind of trumped-up reason that terrorists invariably use to explain an act of murder designed to remove an obstacle to their infamous purpose. However, the infamy of the act brought its own retribution because, although it is not certain that the murderers were ever tried and convicted, from that day the Stern Gang was outlawed and broken up.

Dr Bunche took over as Acting Mediator and throughout the remainder of that year and half-way through the next concluded a series of armistice agreements between the newly-formed Israeli government and her Arab neighbours. As each agreement was promulgated, UN military observers moved into position along the armistice demarcation line. As well as the armistice lines, two demilitarized zones were established, one in the south around El Auja on Israel's border with Egypt, and the other in the north along her border with Syria, between Lake Tiberias and Lake Huleh. It was these demilitarized zones that were to be the greater cause for dispute and violation in the years that followed. This is not surprising, since along the remainder of the demarcation lines Arab faced Jew in direct confrontation, each on his own territory, whereas the demilitarized zones were patrolled and observed only by small UN teams incapable of preventing the determined infiltrator. It is to their credit that they have managed to maintain the reasonable degree of control that they have. But the lesson is clearly learnt that where demilitarized zones are defined, there must be a sufficient UN military presence to supervise them.

The responsibilities of the observers were arduous and exacting. They had to be alert to every violation of the truce and, when these occurred, to report them instantly and accurately so that swift action could be taken to correct the situation and ensure that there was no escalation to a point of fighting. It was no sinecure of a job, no cosy passing of the time in the 'land of milk and honey'. It was a task requiring unceasing vigilance and attention to detail; nor was it without its risks. To be effective the observer needed to be at the scene of any incident before it was over, thereby often exposing himself to the danger of being killed in the exchange of fire. In the circumstances, it is surprising that more were not killed in this way, particularly in UNTSO's early days when neither Arab nor Jew was especially careful whom he shot in the heat of the moment. This was before the days of the blue beret, when the only visible identification worn was an armband on the sleeve of the observer's national uniform.

Despite the danger, the observer teams did not shrink from their responsibilities, but tirelessly investigated complaints of alleged violations and sought a cease-fire wherever the shooting started. They were organized into four Mixed Armistice Commissions (MAC), each being responsible for one of the inter-state armistice lines. Besides the Americans, Belgians and French there were Australians, Canadians, Danes, Irishmen, Italians, Dutchmen, New Zealanders, Norwegians and Swedes. Equipped with a jeep, a radio, a compass, maps and binoculars, the observer relied more than anything else on his own personality, his powers of persuasion and diplomacy for his authority. But most important of all was his ability to be impartial. This is something not easy to achieve to the entire satisfaction of the disputants, particularly when there are as many as in the Middle East. It was not therefore surprising that a number of observers found themselves *persona non grata* because of allegations that they were more partial to one side than to the other. It is one of the peacekeeper's most difficult problems to convince others of his impartiality—only when he is equally unpopular with all parties at the same time can he be sure of satisfying everyone of his absolute impartiality! The tightrope on which he walks every day requires a prodigious balancing act.

Among its Chiefs of Staff UNTSO has had the able but taciturn General Burns of Canada, who when once asked by a press photographer to smile replied, 'Smile! I am smiling, damn it'; the controversial General von Horn of Sweden who also commanded the Congo operation for a while, as well as the observer missions in Lebanon and Yemen before leaving UN service over disagreements with UN Headquarters; and General Odd Bull, who was Chief of Staff from 1963 to 1970—not a Red Indian Chief, as one might imagine from his name, but an eminent Norwegian air force chief!*

3

The Israeli–UAR war of 1956 and the establishment of the United Nations Emergency Force in the Gaza Strip and in Sinai only slightly altered UNTSO's responsibilities, which remained those of supervising the 1949 armistice lines—a task that had been interrupted by Israel's 'eight days' wonder that took her armies to the Suez Canal and the Straits of Tiran on the Red Sea. Her reluctant withdrawal in 1957 to her former frontiers in no way encouraged a greater sense of security and the clashes along the armistice lines continued as before. But with her southern border covered by UNEF it was largely Syria and Jordan that engaged Israel's attention and the observers watching the demarcation lines were kept very busy and alert, operating around the clock. There were 84 observers with the Mixed Armistice Commissions responsible for these two areas,

* During the Second World War, when his country was occupied by the Nazis, General Bull joined the RAF and served with Coastal Command.

commanded by Canadians—Colonels Bertrand and Flint.* There was very little peace in the frontier areas throughout the ten years between the wars, but, though the skirmishing on occasions developed into short artillery and tank battles, the demarcation lines remained intact and were not erased; as they might well have been had not there been a UN presence.

4

In the latter part of 1966 the situation in the north became progressively worse with the intensification of Arab activity. The fedayeen were continuing their raids into Israel from Gaza, but there was a more serious situation developing in the north where infiltrators from Syria carried out a series of terrorist attacks in which many Jews were killed and their property destroyed. Despite Syria's denials there was not much doubt that she was aiding and abetting the terrorists. The Security Council called on her to take stronger steps to prevent the incidents, but they did not abate. A counter-claim by Syria, supported by the USSR, that Israel was massing troops on her border was refuted, there being no evidence to that effect. Fighting between Israel and Jordan also flared up again but the chief area of armed conflict was in the north. Nineteen sixty-seven opened with further clashes across the border. Attempts by the Mixed Armistice Commission to restore order were unsuccessful—there was no real intent on either side to find a settlement. In April occurred the most serious incident yet, which arose over cultivation rights in the demilitarized zone. The Syrians had previously opened fire on Israeli tractors ploughing inside the zones. The Israelis substituted armoured tractors which were then shelled by Syrian artillery. Israeli

* In May 1958, during a skirmish between Israeli police and Jordanian soldiers in the Mount Scopus area of Jerusalem, Colonel Flint was shot and killed when trying to procure a cease-fire.

fighter aircraft attacked the gun positions and were themselves engaged by Syrian fighters, six of which were shot down without loss to the Israelis. This display of air superiority might have been taken as a warning, but by now it was too late. A month later Egypt demanded UNEF's removal in order better to support her Arab ally in the event of an attack by Israel. On 5 June the Israeli Army attacked on all fronts simultaneously and within a week was all-conquering.

The Middle East War of 1967 solved nothing; if anything it made matters more difficult. The confrontation has simply been re-sited along the Suez Canal, the west bank of the river Jordan and the Golan Heights, extending considerably the lines of communication over which UNTSO must maintain observation. Besides her existing responsibilities UNTSO was given the task of policing the Canal front. Initially a team of 20 observers was deployed to cover both banks, but this was clearly inadequate and later the number was increased to 90. Their presence did not prevent the periodic interchange of commando raids across the Canal, nor the almost daily shelling of enemy positions by both sides. On the Jordan front there was a temporary lull while the badly-mauled Jordanian army re-grouped and re-equipped itself; but a new brand of offensive resistance was developing with the upsurge of nationalism among the Palestinian refugees in Jordan, and it was not long before an intense guerrilla war was being fought on the West Bank. Syria took the longest to recover but before long Israel's positions along the Golan Heights were again being threatened.

So the situation has continued. The latest cease-fire, in 1970, has provided an uneasy truce with little calming of tempers. UNTSO is still there and its responsibilities remain unaltered, though in extent they have been increased. In terms of success it might be supposed that it has achieved little. Despite UNTSO's presence, the fighting is forever recurring; certainly in the 22 years of its existence there has been little abatement in the unrest, the skirmishing, the blatant violations of the de-militarized zones. Israel's determination to be recognized and her strong sense of self-preservation have made her suspicious and intransigent in her attitude towards UNTSO; often to the point of being non-co-operative. On the other hand it cannot be said that UNTSO has fared very much better with the Arab states, whose bitter opposition to the Jewish states overrides restraint. But in evaluating UNTSO's contribution to the Middle East crisis, one should start with fundamentals and consider to what extent the purposes for which UNTSO was established were achieved. One should not judge it on whether it prevented war or not—of its very nature, the mandate it was given was one of supervision not prevention. Twice in its exist-ence war has broken out in the Middle East. It is doubtful whether any agency on earth could have averted war at the time; certainly the 'third'-party intervention of Britain and France in 1956 exacerbated, rather than calmed, the situation. But during the years between, the military conflict was restricted to one of skirmishing and raids across the armistice lines—and for this the MAC teams can take much of the credit; nor should it be forgotten that there were many places along the demarca-tion lines that enjoyed comparative if not total quiet throughout these ten-year periods—a circumstance which would not have existed had there been no UNTSO and no UN presence. In a sentence, UNTSO's performance has been one of courageous endeavour.

5

Lebanon 1958

A constitutional crisis in the Lebanon in the summer of 1958 threatened to end in civil war and in open conflict between Lebanon and her own Arab 'allies'. For some time there had been marked dissatisfaction among the Moslem community (approximately half of the $1\frac{1}{2}$ million inhabitants—the other half being Christians) with the Government's apparent pro-Western policies. On 10 May, 1958, a prominent anti-government campaigner, Nassib Mathi, a newspaper proprietor, was murdered, allegedly by government agents. There followed disturbances in the major towns of Beirut, Tripoli and Sidon which increased in violence as the days passed. Several people were killed in the streets during the frequent exchanges of fire; others, mostly innocent people, died in bombing outrages. Among the dead was the nephew of the Army Commander-in-Chief, General Chehab, who later became President in place of President Chamoun. Chamoun had been unpopular with the other Arab states since his refusal to break off relations with Great Britain and France at the time of Suez. Nor did his refusal to include non-Christians in his government endear him to the Moslem world. His declared intention to stand again for the presidency later in the year had contributed to the existing unrest.

Chamoun accused the UAR of being behind the disturbances and Syria, in particular, with aiding and abetting the mass infiltration of armed fighters across her borders into Lebanon. He appealed to the Security Council to consider Lebanon's charges against Egypt and Syria. The Security Council delayed action until the Arab League had had the opportunity to settle the dispute, but when the League proved unsuccessful, it debated the Lebanese situation and on 11 June, adopted a Swedish resolution calling for the immediate despatch of an observer mission, 'to ensure that there is no illegal infiltration of personnel or supply of arms or other *materiel* across the Lebanese border'.

The United Nations Observer Group in Lebanon (UNOGIL) wasted no time in forming. Its top tier was a politico-military triumvirate: Señor Galo Plaza, former President of Ecuador;

General Odd Bull, Norway's former Air Force Chief; and Rajeshwar Dayal of India. Supporting them were more than 200 field observers who were deployed throughout the country and not only along the Syrian border. To increase the Mission's observation capability, it was provided with eight light reconnaissance planes and two helicopters by USA and Sweden— those from America being flown by UN pilots. But UNOGIL's main problem was to gain access to those frontier areas held by dissident tribesmen, into and through which the infiltrations were allegedly being made. The tribes in these areas were on the whole unco-operative, though at times UN observers were allowed to enter under escort. With this handicap and the general difficulty of movement in the mountainous terrain, UNOGIL found its task no easy one, but in its first report, published on 4 July, it stated that it had found no tangible evidence of mass infiltration of arms or of UAR nationals. This report angered President Chamoun, who called it 'inconclusive, misleading and unwarranted'; he added 'if we Lebanese can only tell a Syrian by his dialect, how can a Norwegian or a Swede tell an infiltrator from the Lebanese?' He seems to have missed the point that UNOGIL had reported 'no evidence of mass infiltration'. The Lebanese Government claimed that there were 3,000 Egyptian, Syrian and Palestinian rebels inside borders and that the UAR had supplied the anti-government forces with 36,000 weapons of various kinds; UNOGIL, for all its limitations, including that of identification, found no proof of this, then or later.

On 12 July a new development in the Middle East brought a change in the character of the Lebanese situation. In Iraq, King Faisal and most of the Royal Family were assassinated and a military régime under Brigadier Kassem was proclaimed. First Jordan and then Lebanon reacted strongly. Like them, Iraq under Faisal had been pro-Western and so to them the events of 12 July were ominous indeed. King Hussein appealed to

Britain for military help and President Chamoun did likewise to the United States. Both answered the call and while Britain flew a parachute brigade into Amman, the Americans landed 1,500 marines* across the Lebanese beach, much to the enjoyment of the holiday-makers and tourists who were sunning themselves on the sands or bathing in the sea; while offshore lay a small naval armada of aircraft carriers, heavy cruisers and destroyers.

The intention was a show of force and this is what it remained until the final withdrawal in October. UNOGIL made it clear at once that it would have no working relationship or contact with the US force, since UNOGIL was operating under a specific mandate from the Security Council. It continued therefore to carry out its tasks independently of the altered situation.

On 31 July, General Chehab was elected President,† but resisted any pressure to assume office before Chamoun's term of office ended. This probably prolonged the unrest by a few weeks, for feeling was strong among the Moslems that Chamoun should go at once. But on 23 September Chehab took office and from then onwards, with a better-balanced representation in the government, life began to return to normal. UNOGIL had made a second report in July which basically confirmed the first that there was no evidence to support the claim of massive smuggling of arms or armed rebels. Despite the difficulties of observation, over 100 allegations had been investigated but in no case had there been explicit confirmation of the complaint to warrant further action by UNOGIL. In short, though smuggling and infiltration was almost certainly going on, it was clearly on a relatively small scale and confined to small arms and ammunition. When UNOGIL came to render its third and fourth reports, this opinion was maintained.

On 22 November, with Lebanon relatively quiet once again,

---

* To be increased to 10,000 troops by 20 July.
† President Chamoun had earlier announced that he would not after all seek re-election.

UNOGIL began its withdrawal, completing it on 10 December. In its six months' existence it had played an important calming role and, so far as its mandate was concerned, had satisfactorily rebutted the allegations made in the first instance by Chamoun and the Lebanese Government, showing them to have been greatly exaggerated. UNOGIL's presence may not have prevented smuggling and infiltration, but it had ensured that they were kept within limited bounds.

6

Yemen 1963–64

If any one of the United Nations' operations is to be classed as a failure, this is it; but it was a failure in implementation rather than in performance. There were three fundamental reasons for this. First, from the beginning those countries concerned in the dispute disregarded their promises to implement the terms of the truce agreed with the Secretary-General's Representative, Dr Ralph Bunche. Bunche had gone to the Yemen early in 1963 to try and find a solution to the civil war that had been raging since the previous September. Second, Egypt and Saudi Arabia, who had undertaken to meet the costs of the UN operation for the first two months, later withheld further payments even though it was largely because of them that the period of the UN mission had to be extended. Third, the terrain was probably the most difficult that a UN observer mission had ever encountered—the high massif to the north and east making effective observation over the area well-nigh impossible. The difficulties might have been eased had Saudi Arabia fulfilled her promise to co-operate in checking the flow of arms to the Imam's forces—the Royalists.

The Yemen is peopled by two distinct religious sects, the Zaidi and the Shafi. After the expulsion of the Turks in 1917 the

Zaidis held power under their temporal and spiritual leader, the Imam. In September 1962, the old Imam, Ahmad, died and was succeeded by his son, Imam Badr. Ahmad had been an autocratic and despotic king who had ruled by suppression. He had survived more than one attempt to overthrow him. His son was more liberal and constitutionally-minded and promised to undertake a policy of modern reform. But he was not to be given the opportunity. Only a week after his accession, a military revolt drove him from his throne. The rebels, led by a former prisoner of Ahmad, Colonel Sallal,* numbered among their ranks both Zaidis and Shafis. Sallal was himself a Zaidi. It was a typical military coup in which the royal palace in the capital, Sana'a, was surrounded by tanks and shelled into ruins. At first it was supposed that Badr lay dead among the rubble along with the rest of his family and royal bodyguard, but he managed to escape and, dressed as an ordinary soldier, fled to the mountainous north, the stronghold of the loyal Zaidi tribes. Here, with the assistance of King Faisal of Saudi Arabia, he collected around himself an army and prepared to wage war against the new republic that Colonel (now Field-Marshal) Sallal had proclaimed.

Throughout the next few months fighting between the two rival groups was widespread and intense with each side claiming victories. The situation was confused but by the end of the year the two groups remained entrenched and firm in their respective areas, the Royalists (Badr) in the mountains of the north and in the east, along the borders with Saudi Arabia and the Republicans (Sallal) in the large towns and in the south. But Egypt was supplying Sallal with an increasing amount of material support. By January it was reported that there were between twelve and twenty-two thousand UAR troops in the Yemen and this figure was later to exceed 25,000. With Saudi

* It was said that he had been held in solitary confinement for seven years.

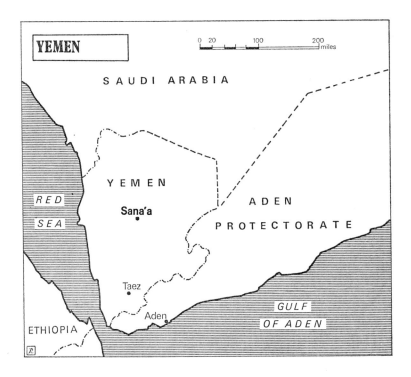

Arabia strongly supporting the Imam, it looked like being a long war. International pressures failed to deter either Nasser or Faisal from interfering.

In March 1963, Bunche went to the Yemen on a fact-finding mission for the Secretary-General. As a result of his visit and others to Cairo and Riyadh, he was able to get agreement to a peace formula. Saudi Arabia would terminate all aid to the Royalists and bar the use of her territory to their leaders. On her part, the UAR would begin a phased withdrawal of her forces from the Yemen—she also undertook not to take punitive action against the Royalists on Saudi Arabian territory. A demilitarized zone was to be established, extending 20 kilometres on each side of Yemen's border with Saudi Arabia. It was recommended that UN observers should be stationed inside the demilitarized zone to ensure that there was no infiltration of troops or arms across it. They would be required to verify the withdrawal of the UAR troops and the cessation of royalist activity inside Saudi Arabia. They would check outside the zone where necessary on disengagement progress. This plan of disengagement, evolved after Bunche's visit and a further mediatory effort by Ellsworth Bunker,* was a constructive effort towards a peaceful settlement and could well have succeeded had there been any display of good faith on the part of the involved parties to implement the terms of the agreement. The fact that they did not, made the task of any UN observer mission largely ineffectual.

The United Nations Observer Mission (UNYOM) arrived in the Yemen on 13 June, 1963. Its mandate was for four months. It was 200 strong, of which the largest single elements were a reconnaissance unit from Yugoslavia and an air component of 50 from Canada, operating 8 reconnaissance aircraft. Others came from India, Italy, Denmark, Netherlands, Ghana, Norway, Sweden and Pakistan, withdrawn from the UN operations in the Congo and Middle East. Head of the Mission was General von Horn, who had been moved from UNTSO to take on this new commitment; his place as UNTSO's Chief of Staff being taken by General Bull. Von Horn had paid an advance visit to the Yemen for consultations and reconnaissance and was far from sanguine about the Mission's chances of success.

The presence of UNYOM made little difference to the situation in the Yemen; fighting continued and the terms of the agreement were not honoured. Being no party to the agreement, the Royalists ignored it and UNYOM. The UAR made only token withdrawals of its troops and on occasions replaced those that it had withdrawn. Saudi Arabia, allegedly because of the UAR's non-compliance with its part of the agreement, did not

* See p. 91.

desist from aiding the Royalists and took no action to halt the traffic of men and arms across the border. Inside the demilitarized zone itself all was relatively quiet, so much so that by November 1964, U Thant was able to recommend the withdrawal of the Mission's one military unit, the Yugoslav reconnaissance unit. This left some 25 observers for the task of checking and observing how the agreement was or was not being implemented. The truth was that it was not, but the limitations on the scope and size of the Mission were such that it was really acting in a vacuum in which whatever it did or said it was disregarded. Having proceeded along this abortive and unproductive road for fifteen months, the Mission was eventually withdrawn and disbanded in September 1964.

Everything was against UNYOM from the start—bad faith, terrain and financial provision. The Yemen experience leads one to question the advisability of mounting a peace effort of inadequate dimensions, and to consider the desirability of terminating a military observer mission if it becomes obvious that it is no longer an effective instrument for peace, when the policies of the disputants continue to run contrary to the initial agreements, for the supervision of which the UN mission was established in the first place. The Yemen operation may have been a failure but the plan for which it was designed was not.

7

India–Pakistan 1949–71

Of all its operations, that of the UN in Kashmir is the one that has been heard of least, though it has been in existence for as long as UNTSO. The fact that after 22 years the United Nations Military Observer Group in India and Pakistan (UNMOGIP) is still performing its duties along the Kashmir cease-fire line and in doing so underwrites the continuing peace in that state, is something that is forgotten by most of

the world. There is no news value where there are no
fireworks and so long as UNMOGIP continues to keep
the peace successfully, it and Kashmir will remain out
of the newspapers and will go on being forgotten. Since,
unlike other UN missions and peacekeeping forces, UNMOGIP
does not submit regular reports on the Kashmir scene,
there is no periodic reminder of its existence. For diplomatic
and political reasons it was felt advisable at the beginning
to confine reporting to private rather than public channels.
This was considered desirable because in Kashmir the military
observers were constantly being required in the course of their

duties to switch from one side of the cease-fire line to the other and back again; allegations of partiality and bias by either side could have greatly hindered their work. Later, when Dr Frank Graham was appointed the Secretary-General's Representative, the practice was continued so as not to jeopardize or embarass his peace efforts. However advisable this policy of quiet diplomacy was thought to be at the time, it did not help to alert the General Assembly to the deterioration in the inter-state relations that brought about the India–Pakistan war of 1965.

8

The Kashmir dispute dates from 1947, the year in which India was partitioned and she and Pakistan received their independence. Up to this time the Indian princes had ruled autonomous states, but now they were required to accede to one or the other of the two new Dominions. Kashmir was one of a few that did not opt either way. A predominantly Muslin state, her ruler, Maharajah Sir Hari Singh, was a Hindu. In August 1947, when a revolt in the town of Poonch was suppressed by the State forces, the Muslim tribesmen of neighbouring North-West Frontier Province (Pakistan), incensed by reports that their Kashmiri brothers were being massacred, invaded Kashmir to go to their assistance. Whether or not there was massacre before, there certainly was now, with pillaging and murder on a substantial scale. The Maharaja appealed to India for help and received it—but in return for his state's accession. On 27 October, 1947, Indian army units crossed the border into Kashmir.

The fighting that followed was bitter and costly. Diplomatic manoeuvres by both sides at first failed to bring the issue to the United Nations, but in January 1948, both agreed to a UN Commission to look into the dispute. Inexplicably the Commission (UNCIP) did not reach Kashmir until three months later, by which time the situation had further deteriorated. India claimed that there were 50,000 rebels in Kashmir and another 100,000 being trained in Pakistan, but the real issue was over the timing of the people's plebiscite which would decide Kashmir's future. India wanted it held while the newly-appointed government remained in power, but since the Prime Minister, Sheikh Abdullah, was known to oppose Kashmir's union with Pakistan, the latter saw little likelihood of an impartial plebiscite in such circumstances and advocated that it be held under UN auspices.

UNCIP had to wait almost a year before it saw any return for its efforts. In January 1949, a cease-fire was arranged but its continuance rested on good-will, for there was as yet no agreement on an armistice. However, later in the same month UNCIP succeeded in bringing the two army commanders together, having failed with the politicians.* In July, after further military meetings, the Karachi Agreement was signed. By it a formal cease-fire came into effect along a mutually agreed cease-fire line, which would be supervised by UN observers stationed on both sides of it.

UNMOGIP was responsible both for supervising the cease-fire and for adjudicating in cases of alleged violations of the Karachi Agreement. Until the India–Pakistan war of 1965 the number of military observers did not exceed 50 at any one time. An additional 59 were provided during that crisis, but otherwise this relatively small band of observers from eleven countries† has prevented a breach of the armistice during the time it has been in effect. The fact that few people outside of Asia and the contributing countries know of its existence is a measure of its success. Numerous allegations and incidents

---

* It is of interest that the officer signing the official minutes of this meeting on behalf of Pakistan's British C-in-C was Lt-Col A. J. Wilson, then on the GHQ staff. Six years later he was to become Chief of Staff of UNFICYP, prior to the author.

† See Appendix A.

were investigated in the period between 1949 and 1965. Each one was meticulously examined and in the majority of cases an adjudication made against one side or the other. Each has been recorded and reported, not only to the governments of both sides but also to the Secretary-General. As a deterrent to escalation UNMOGIP has been most effective.

9

In 1965, however, UNMOGIP was rendered temporarily ineffective by the India–Pakistan war that broke the cease-fire agreement and threatened the peace of Asia once again. Early in the year, fighting broke out in the Rann of Kutch, a sector of the border between India and Pakistan that had been in dispute for some time. Essentially it was over a territorial claim which was eventually settled by an international tribunal headed by Judge Lagergen of Sweden, which allocated 10% of the disputed area to Pakistan and the remainder to India—but that was in 1968, well after the cease-fire had been re-established. During the first six months of 1965 the number of violations of the cease-fire line multiplied to almost 400—from crossings to artillery exchanges. During August and September major engagements took place in which tanks and aircraft, as well as artillery, took part. Both armies made advances across the cease-fire line and also across the international frontier in places. But determined efforts by the UN succeeded in arranging a cease-fire on 22 September, 1965, and although it was broken on occasions during the succeeding months, the infringements were minor and did not bring about a renewal of the fighting.

On 20 September, when negotiations for a cease-fire were nearing conclusion, the Security Council authorized the Secretary-General to provide an additional observer group for outside Kashmir after hostilities ceased. It was established immediately the cease-fire took effect and remained in existence until March of the following year, its purpose by then having been served. The United Nations India–Pakistan Observer Mission (UNIPOM) had the role of supervising the cease-fire along the international frontiers and observing the military withdrawals by both sides, back within their own boundaries. UNIPOM was 82 strong and was deployed almost equally on either side of the frontier. It was commanded by Major-General Bruce Macdonald of Canada who previously had been Deputy Chief of Staff in UNFICYP. When it departed, having completed its task, it left UNMOGIP to continue its duties in Kashmir, where it still is to-day—keeping peace where no peaceful solution has yet been found.

CHAPTER 7

Korea
1950-1953

I

It may well be wondered why the United Nations operations in Korea should have been left to the last—added almost as a postscript to the rest. It is not that the Korean war lacked significance; quite the contrary, it represents the first and only time that member states of the United Nations have allied themselves under the strict terms of the Charter to oppose a threat to international peace. But a greater significance lies in how the war came to be fought, not how it was fought; it is this that qualifies it for a place in this book, not so much the fighting which conformed with the progress of most other wars, as the map showing its four phases so clearly indicates. It is improbable that such action by the United Nations will ever be taken again, which makes Korea unique in the annals of UN peace-keeping and which makes its origins more interesting than the campaign itself. In saying this, it is not meant to belittle the contribution made by those countries that formed the UN Force—their contribution was considerable and proved how possible it is for a quickly assembled international army to operate successfully under the leadership of one of its member countries. I hope the reader will allow me to leave it there and to concentrate on the antecedents of this unique UN experience.

2

In 1949, after attempts to unite the country had failed, separate elections were held in North and South Korea setting up two independent systems of government. In the north there had

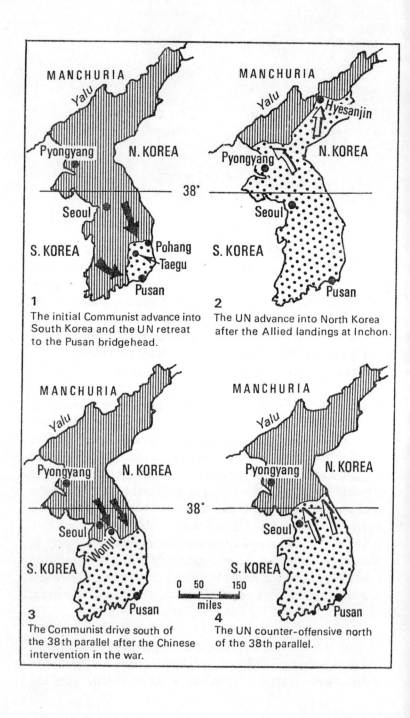

1
The initial Communist advance into
South Korea and the UN retreat
to the Pusan bridgehead.

2
The UN advance into North Korea
after the Allied landings at Inchon.

3
The Communist drive south of
the 38th parallel after the Chinese
intervention in the war.

4
The UN counter-offensive north
of the 38th parallel.

been a Russian occupation force since Japan's surrender in 1945 and it was not surprising that North Korea became a communist state. In the south, where the USA had maintained a similar force, the elections were more democratic despite efforts by the Reds to sabotage them. A UN Commission (UNTCOK) had been in the country since early 1948 for the purpose of observing the elections but had been denied any access to the north. The dividing line between the two occupation forces was the 38th parallel of latitude. In the first half of 1950 America and Russia withdrew their forces and the South and North Koreans were left facing each other across this abstract frontier. It did not remain abstract for long for on 25 June, 1950, North Korea invaded the South. The following day South Korea appealed to the United States for military assistance and on the 27th the Security Council adopted a resolution recommending 'that the Member States furnish such assistance to the Republic of Korea as may be necessary to repel the armed attack and to restore international peace and security in the area'. The adoption of such a resolution would have been out of the question had the Russian delegate been present in the Council to wield his power of veto, but he was not—he had been absent since the previous January when he walked out in protest against the Nationalist Chinese permanent member of the Council being seated as Chairman in his rightful turn.

Since it was largely due to the Russian walk-out that UN armed intervention in Korea became possible, the circumstances of that walk-out should be more specifically described. The procedure within the Security Council is that the representative of each of the permanent member states of the Council, China, France, the United Kingdom, the United States and the USSR, take the chair in rotation for a period of one month. On this occasion it was the turn of China, represented in the United Nations by the delegate of General Chiang Kai-shek's Nationalist Government, Dr T. S. Tsiang. When he took his place on

10 January, 1950, the Russian delegate, Mr Malik, immediately challenged his credibility as the representative of China in the UN, claiming that he was only the representative of the Kuomintang and not of the Republic of China led by Mao Tse-tung. This apparently long-overdue disclaimer by the Russians that they did not recognize the validity of Nationalist China's membership of the Council had been precipitated by a letter received shortly before by the Secretary-General from Premier Chou En-lai to the effect that the People's Government of the Republic of China held as illegal the presence of the delegate of Nationalist China in the Council and demanded that he should be expelled. Malik now made it clear that 'if the Council fails to take the appropriate measures for the exclusion from its membership of the representative of the Kuomintang group, the delegation of the USSR will not participate in the work of the Council'. He followed this by presenting a short resolution to that effect. In reply Dr Tsiang, speaking as the Council's presiding President, ruled that Mr Malik's proposal be printed and circulated to the other members for subsequent consideration. This did not satisfy the Russians who were looking for a quick kill; Malik maintaining that he could not accept a ruling from a President he did not recognize. Tsiang declared that his ruling was being challenged and asked the Council to vote upon it. As was to be expected, the vote strongly supported Tsiang's ruling that Malik's proposal should be committed to writing. Since the issue was one of procedure, the USSR's negative vote did not count as a veto. Two days later, at the next Council meeting, the USSR proposal was debated. It was defeated by six votes to three with two abstentions. Malik, after delivering a strong condemnation of the Council's vote, left the chamber with his entire delegation and was not to return to it for eight months, by which time the UN Force was well established in Korea. Because of the USSR's withdrawal the communist world was deprived of its power to veto decisions of the Security

Council. Only permanent members could exercise the veto; so although Yugoslavia sat in the Security Council as a rotational member she had no power to veto. The resolution calling on all member states to go to South Korea's assistance therefore passed through unhindered. It is difficult to imagine similar circumstances presenting themselves again.

3

Another exception to UN peacekeeping procedure to date was for the direction and command of an operation to be delegated to someone other than the Secretary-General. In all other instances it has been the Secretary-General who has been in charge. But on this occasion the responsibility was given to an American General and the US Joint Chief of Staff's Committee —an expedient possibly thought necessary since the USA was supplying the bulk of the troops. In fact the proportion of Americans to others was such that it is sometimes difficult not to think of the Korean war was anything but an American venture under the cloak of the United Nations—though a glance at the list of contributing nations disproves this. America's manpower contribution included three Army Corps, a Marine Division, a Naval carrier force and other naval units, and a Tactical and Bomber air force. The second largest contingent came from the United Kingdom and Commonwealth countries, who between them formed the famous Commonwealth Division and provided sizeable naval and air support. Belgium, Colombia, Cuba, Ethiopia, France, Greece, Luxembourg, The Netherlands, The Philippines, Thailand and Turkey all contributed ground forces, while Denmark, India, Norway and Sweden contributed medical units. Great Britain was early in Korea, deploying part of her Far East force, based on Hong Kong and Singapore. Later Britain's land force contribution was increased to two infantry brigades, an armoured regiment and a regiment of artillery.

As the map shows, the initial thrust by the North Korean army invested the whole of the South except for a small bridge-head around Pusan, through which it was possible to pass rein-forcement units to build up the UN strength. By the middle of July the Americans were fighting tenaciously to maintain a foothold on the mainland. But as the strain on the North Koreans' lines of communication increased as the UN's air offensive built up and as the UN land forces were strengthened, the initiative began to shift and the North Koreans to withdraw northwards. For the next four months they were driven back inexorably across the 38th Parallel to the Yalu River on the very borders of China itself. But with the total defeat of the North Korean army in sight, the Chinese Republic came to its assist-ance, and at the end of November 1950, Phase III of the cam-paign began with the communist forces driving south once again. It is estimated that the Chinese deployed up to 7 army corps, totalling 21 divisions and 200,000 men, in Korea. It is not surprising therefore that the UN army was forced to give way under the initial assault. The communist advance, con-tested every inch of the way, was eventually halted south of Seoul; it had been a costly operation and the casualties on both sides had been extremely heavy, but this was to be the end of the road so far as the communists were concerned. Early in 1951 Inchon and Seoul were freed. By 31 March the 38th Parallel was recrossed. Heavy counter-attacks by the communists, with serious losses to both sides, were successfully repulsed. In July negotiations for a cease-fire began but it was not until July 1953, two years later, that a cease-fire was arranged and an armistice agreement signed. Like so many wars of the past, the agreed armistice line conformed very nearly to the former de-marcation line—a form of territorial *status quo ante*. Casualty figures ran into millions. Over 300,000 South Koreans and

140,000 Americans were killed, wounded or were missing, plus another 14,000 from the other member states—from these figures alone it can be seen to what extent the USA bore the brunt. Of the communists, it is estimated that there were between $1\frac{1}{2}$ and 2 million casualties; and an untold number of civilians.

The Armistice Commissions still continue their duties to-day on either side of the 38th Parallel. Occasionally, there are breaches of the cease-fire and soldiers die—American or Chinese. It is an uneasy truce which, but for the continued presence of the Commissions, could very easily burst again into hot-blooded war. The United Nations' armed intervention did serve its purpose in preventing an escalation into international conflict—but at a heavy price in human life. It is possible that a peaceable intervention, in the manner of UNEF, along the 38th Parallel would have had a comparable result—without that price?

CHAPTER 8

Conclusions

Nobody knows better than the UN peacekeepers and observers themselves how much room there is for improvement. The machinery of international peacekeeping was constructed 26 years ago and so far has remained unmodified, but the structure of the United Nations has changed radically since the day when the Charter was originally drafted. In their wisdom, the founder-members stipulated in the Charter* that there should be a review of its provisions after ten years. Such a review has been considered but so far has not taken place; there are those who believe that changes would not necessarily improve the Charter. The likelihood of a review is slight in the present political climate; any alteration would require a two-thirds majority of an all-member vote and the chances of obtaining this would be remote. Accepting, therefore, that a Charter revision is out of the question—at least within the foreseeable future—what is there that can be done to strengthen the weaknesses in the existing machinery and to make it operationally more effective?

So far as the procedural machinery within the United Nations is concerned, three possibilities present themselves:

(1) The Charter itself is broad in its directions regarding the use of peacekeeping forces. To apply these effectively there needs to be a set of Standing Procedures or a Statement of Guiding Principles which the Security Council could use for mounting and developing peace initiatives. These procedures or principles, while being consistent with the Charter itself, would help to remedy the existing anomalies

* Articles 108–109.

by ensuring that the implementing of the Council's authority for peacekeeping would remain constantly in tune with modern times and would meet the requirements of progressive development and change—thereby providing greater flexibility of initiative. They would in no way challenge the overriding authority of the Charter, but whereas it might not be practicable or desirable to revise the latter, the procedures or principles could be subject to adjustment.

(2) The provision of an 'early warning system' in the form of an advisory group to the Security Council could alert its members sooner to the potential areas of conflict in the world. In doing so, the group could focus attention on the build-up of tension in a particular part of the world so that the Security Council would be better prepared to moderate the dangerous tendencies before they went beyond the point of prevention. A somewhat similar recommendation was made in the United Nations by Brazil, but she set the advisory group within the department of the Under-Secretary-General for Special Political Affairs. It is doubtful whether this positioning of the group would be acceptable to the Security Council.

(3) The establishment of a contingency planning staff to mount and co-ordinate all peacekeeping operations and observer missions. It should be a joint civilian/military staff with a civilian chairman (to underline the fact that the responsibility for mounting UN peacekeeping forces and missions is a civilian not a military one). Its military members could be in a purely advisory capacity but their presence on the staff is essential to the understanding of the military operational requirements of whichever force or mission it is.

So much for the procedure; now for the execution. It should not be thought that the problems would end with the implementation of ideas such as those above. The *ad hoc* nature of peacekeeping and the unwritten requirement that the force/ mission must be acceptable to the host country remain stumbling blocks to full effectiveness. The first can to a large extent be overcome by training; not the national training of earmarked troops in individual countries, but by joint training in geographical regional groups and on a transnational basis. The extremes of experience and training are great, some of the soldiers that have been involved in past peacekeeping operations have been deficient in training and discipline. An interchange of experience and military know-how could greatly help in the preparation of UN contingents and reduce the degree of operational and administrative chaos that is the feature of most *ad hoc* ventures—for in the field of UN operations everyone is a learner, even the most sophisticated and best-trained professional soldiers.

The problems of acceptability and consent must not be allowed to impose too rigid a constraint upon UN peacekeeping. A 'host' country, in appealing for or consenting to a UN presence, should not be permitted to carry its objection to this or that country's participation beyond a reasonable or justifiable point—otherwise the problems of the Congo, where at one moment the UN Secretariat was literally scraping the barrel to find contingents that were acceptable, will be repeated. Similarly, there should be agreed undertakings at the outset to safeguard against the precipitous removal of a peace force on demand by the host country. The experience of UNEF underlines the need for a notice period before a UN force is withdrawn. None of this denies to the host country its sovereign right to exercise its recognized option if it so wishes, but it does strengthen the UN's authority—an authority necessary to its peacekeeping role.

One clear lesson that has been learnt from UNEF, ONUC and UNFICYP is that the professional soldier, for all his basic military qualities, is not necessarily the best peacekeeper. The non-professional, the volunteer reservist or conscript can in his own right, be every bit as good. There are valid reasons for believing this. First, the man is a volunteer, which gives him a genuine *raison d'être* for being there. Second, it is often the case that he has served previous engagements in the service of the United Nations and has thereby acquired a 'touch'. Third, the non-professionals come from every walk of life—the school-room, the farm, the work bench, the garage, the grocery store, and in doing so have a common bond with those of the community they have come to serve. In this field of human relations, so vital to the work and achievements of a peace force, this built-in source of mutual understanding can often overcome otherwise insuperable obstacles and encourage in the minds of the community itself a more positive and helpful attitude towards the peacekeepers. The professional soldier has much to offer but not everything. The knowledge and experience he can bring to the art of peacekeeping is immense, but a process of adaption is necessary if it is to be successfully applied. The amateur can make a different contribution, but one which is equally valuable.

But training of the military alone is not enough. Peacekeeping/ peacemaking is an operation of 'jointmanship'. Equally, the preparation must be training in jointmanship—not only between diplomats, soldiers and the civil servants of the secretariat, but also with the other professionals and specialists that are needed for the reconstruction of community life, the doctors, engineers, technicians of all kinds and the voluntary services. All agencies have a place, and what past experience has established is the need for an integrated effort involving the soldier peacekeeper, the diplomat peacemaker, the civil servant administrator and, by no means least, the 'professionals' of reconstruction, both social and structural.

If I have done nothing else by this book, perhaps I will have evoked among those who read it a realization that there is nothing to replace the peacekeeping machine of the United

Nations—no national, no international, no transnational substitute. If I have, then I will be satisfied. It is essential that the machinery be made as workable as possible. The will of the international community must be aroused on matters of vital future interest to the world—including the role of United Nations peacekeeping in restricting and ending violence, in helping to create the conditions in which change can take place peacefully and just settlements can be reached.

BIBLIOGRAPHY

Books

United Nations Organisation—General

BOYD, ANDREW: *Fifteen Men on a Powder Keg: A History of the U.N. Security Council*. Methuen, London, 1971.

CORDIER, ANDREW W. and FOOTE, WILDER: *The Quest for Peace* (The Dag Hammarskjöld Memorial Lectures). Columbia University Press, New York and London, 1965.

COYLE, D. C.: *The United Nations and How It Works*. Mentor Books, New York, 1965.

ECKSTEIN, HARRY (ed.): *Internal Wars: Problems and Approaches*. Free Press of Clencoe, New York, 1964.

GLICK, E. B.: *Peaceful Conflict*. Stackpole Books, Harrisburg, Pa, 1967.

GOODRICH, LELAND M. and HAMBRO, EDWARD: *Charter of the United Nations: Commentary and Documents*. World Peace Foundation, Boston, 1949.

GOODRICH, LELAND M.: *The United Nations*. Thomas Y. Crowell, New York, 1959.

GROSS, ERNEST A.: *The United Nations Structure for Peace*. Harper Bros, New York, 1962.

HASLUK, PAUL: *Workshops of Security*. F. W. Cheshire, Melbourne, 1948.

KELEN, EMERY: *Peace is an Adventure*. Meredith Papers, New York, 1967.

NICHOLAS, H. G.: *The U.N. as a Political Institution*. Oxford University Press, London, 1959.

LIE, TRYGVE: *In the Cause of Peace*. Macmillan, New York, 1954.

LUARD, EVAN: *Conflict and Peace in the Modern International System*. Little, Brown, 1968; ULP, 1970.

MARTIN, A. and EDWARDS, J. B. S.: *The Changing Charter*. Sylvan Press, London, 1955.

TETLOW, EDWIN: *The United Nations—The First 25 Years.* Peter Owen, London, 1970.

UNITED NATIONS: *General Assembly Official Records* (GAOR) 1946 ff. New York: United Nations 1947 ff.

UNITED NATIONS: *Security Council Official Records* (SCOR) 1946 ff. New York: United Nations 1947 ff.

UNITED NATIONS SECRETARIAT: *Annual Report of the Secretary-General on the Work of the Organization,* 1946 ff. New York: United Nations 1947 ff.

WEISSBERG, GUENTER: *The International Status of the United Nations.* Oceana Publications, New York, 1963.

U.N. Peacekeeping—Military Forces and International Policing

BLOOMFIELD, LINCOLN and OTHERS: *International Military Forces.* Little, Brown & Co. (Canada) Ltd, 1964.

BOWETT, DEREK: *United Nations Forces,* London, 1964.

BURNS, ARTHUR LEE and HEATHCOTE, NINA: *Peacekeeping by U.N. Forces: From Suez to the Congo.* Praeger, New York, 1963.

CALVOCCORESSI, PETER: *World Order and New States.* Praeger, New York, 1962. Chatto & Windus (Institute for Strategic Studies), London, 1962.

COX, A. M.: *Prospects for Peacekeeping.* Brookings Institution, Washington DC, 1967.

FABIAN, LARRY: *Soldiers without Enemies.* Brookings Institution, 1971.

FRYE, WILLIAM R.: *A United Nations Peace Force.* Oceana Publications, New York, 1957.

GOODRICH, LELAND M. and SIMONS, ANNE P.: *The United Nations and the Maintenance of International Peace and Security.* Brookings Institution, Washington DC, 1955.

HANNING, HUGH: *The Peaceful Uses of Military Forces.* Praeger, New York, 1967.

JAMES, A.: *The Politics of Peacekeeping*. Praeger, New York, 1969.

LUARD, EVAN: *Conflict and Peace in the Modern International System*. Little, Brown & Co. 1968. University of London Press, 1970.

LUARD, EVAN: *Peace and Opinion*. Oxford University Press, London, 1962.

NORWEGIAN INSTITUTE OF INTERNATIONAL AFFAIRS: *Peacekeeping: Experience and evaluation—the Oslo papers*. Hegland boktrykkeri Flekkefjord, 1964

RUSSELL, RUTH B.: *United Nations Experience with Military Forces: Political and Legal Aspects*. Brookings Institution, Washington DC, 1964.

SEYERSTED, F.: *United Nations Forces in the Law of Peace and War*. Sijthoff, Leyden, 1966.

WASKOW, ARTHUR I. and OTHERS: *Quis Custodiet? Controlling the Police in a Disarmed World* (2 vols). Peace Research Institute Inc., Washington, 1963.

WEHBERG, HANS: *Theory and Practice of International Policing*. Constable, London, 1935.

U.N. Peacemaking—Mediation and Negotiation

BAILEY, SYDNEY D.: *Peaceful Settlement of Disputes*. UNITAR paper edn.

BURTON, J. W.: *Conflict and Communication*. Macmillan, London, 1969.

BURTON, J. W.: *Systems, States, Diplomacy and Rules*. Cambridge, 1968.

CÔT, JEAN-PIERRE: *La Conciliation Internationale*. Pedone, Paris, 1968.

DEUTSCH, K. W.: *The Analysis of International Relations*. Prentice-Hall, Englewood Cliffs, N.J., 1968.

FISHER, ROGER: *International Conflict for Beginners*. New York, 1969.

FRANK, JEROME: *Sanity and Survival.* New York, 1968.
LALL, ARTHUR, *Modern International Negotiation.* Columbia, 1966.
MILLER, LINDA B.: *Dynamics of World Politics.* Prentice-Hall, Englewood Cliffs, N. J., 1968.
WALTZ, KENNETH N.: *Man, the States and War.* Columbia, 1965.

U.N. Peacekeeping—Legal Aspects

BARKUN, MICHAEL: *Law Without Sanctions.* Yale, 1968.
BOWETT, D. W.: *United Nations Forces: A Legal Study.* Praeger, New York, 1964.
CLARK, GRENVILLE and SOHN, LOUIS: *World Peace Through World Law.* Harvard University Press, Cambridge, Mass., 1958.
HIGGINS, ROSALYN: *International Law and the United Nations.* Oxford University Press, London, 1963.
KELSEN, HANS: *The Law of the United Nations.* Stevens & Sons Ltd., London, 1951.

U.N. Peacekeeping—Financing

PADELFORD, NORMAN J.: *The Financing of Future Peace and Security Operations Under the U.N.* Brookings Institution, Washington DC, 1962.
STOESSINGER, JOHN G.: *Financing of U.N. Peace and Security Operations.* Brookings Institution, Washington DC, 1962.
STOESSINGER, JOHN G.: *Financing the United Nations System.* Brookings Institution, Washington DC, 1964.

U.N.—Dag Hammarskjöld

HAMMARSKJÖLD, DAG: *Markings.* Knopf, New York, 1964. Faber & Faber, London, 1964.

LASH, JOSEPH P.: Dag Hammarskjöld: *Custodian of the Brushfire Peace*. Doubleday, New York, 1961. Cassell, London, 1962.
MILLER, RICHARD I.: *Dag Hammarskjöld and Crisis Diplomacy*. Oceana Publications, New York, 1961.
THORPE, DERYCK: *Hammarskjöld: Man of Peace*. Stockwell, Ilfracombe, Devon, 1970.

U.N. Peacekeeping—Middle East Operations

AFIFI, MOHAMMED EL-HADI: *The Arabs and the United Nations*. Ontario, 1964.
BURNS, E. L. M.: *Between Arab and Israeli*. Ivan Obolensky, London, 1962. New York, 1963.
HIGGINS, ROSALYN: *United Nations Peacekeeping: 1946–1967. Documents and Commentary. Vol. I—The Middle East*. Oxford University Press, for Institute of International Affairs, 1969.
KLINE, E. O.: *The Suez Crisis*. University of Michigan Press, Ann Arbor, 1962.
LALL, ARTHUR: *The U.N. and the Middle East Crisis*. Columbia, 1970.
ROSNER, GABRIELLA: *The United Nations Emergency Force*. Columbia University Press, New York, 1963.
STILLMAN, A. M.: *The U.N. and the Suez Canal*. University of Michigan Press, Ann Arbor, 1966.
THOMAS, HUGH: *Suez*. Weidenfeld & Nicholson, London, 1967. Harper & Row, New York, 1967.
BAR-YAACOV, N.: *The Israel–Syrian Armistice; Problems of Implementation 1946–66*. Jerusalem, 1967.
BERNADOTTE, FOLKE: *To Jerusalem*. London, 1951.
BROOK, DAVID: *Preface to Peace: the United Nations and the Arab–Israel Armistice System*. Washington, 1964.
HAMZEH, F. S.: *International Conciliation* (with Special Reference to the Work of the United Nations Conciliation Commission for Palestine). Drukkerij Pasmans, The Hague, 1963.

VON HORN, Major General CARL: *Soldiering for Peace*. David McKay, New York, 1967.

WAINHOUSE, D. W.: *International Peace Observation*. Johns Hopkins, Baltimore, 1966.

U.N. Peacekeeping—Congo Operation

ALEXANDER, Major General H. T.: *African Tightrope*. Praeger, New York, 1966.

ALPORT, LORD: *The Sudden Assignment*. Hodder & Stoughton, London, 1965.

BIRNBAUM, KARL E. and SPARRING, ÅKE: *Kongokrisen och FN*. Rabén & Sjögren, Stockholm, 1961.

BORRI, MICHEL: *Nous Ces Affreux* (Dossier Secret de L'Ex-Congo Belge. Editions Galic, Paris, 1962.

BLOOMFIELD, LINCOLN P. (ed.): *International Military Forces*. Little, Brown & Co., Boston, 1964.

BOWETT, D. W.: *United Nations Forces: A Legal Study*. Praeger, New York, 1964.

BOYD, ANDREW: *U.N.—Piety, Myth and Truth*. Penguin, 1962.

CALDER, PETER RITCHIE: *The Agony of the Congo*. Gollancz, London, 1961.

CARTER, GWENDOLYN M. (ed.): *Five African States: Responses to Diversity*. Cornell University Press, Ithaca, 1963.

CENTRE DE RECHERCHE ET D'INFORMATION SOCIO-POLITIQUES: Congo: 1959 (1960, 1961, 1962, 1963, 1964). Edited: J. Gerard-Libois and Benoit Verhaegen: Les Dossiers du C.R.I.S.P., Brussels, 1960–65.

CORNEVIN, ROBERT: *Histoire du Congo (Leopoldville)*. Berger-Levrault, Paris, 1963.

DALLIN, ALEXANDER: *The Soviet Union at the United Nations*. Praeger, New York, 1962.

DAVISTER, PIERRE: *Katanga: enjeu du monde*. Editions Remarques Congolaises, Brussels, 1961.

DINANT, GEORGES: *L'O.N.U. face à la Crise congolaise.* Editions Remarques Congolaises, Brussels, 1961.

EPSTEIN, HOWARD M. (ed.): *Revolt in the Congo: 1960–64.* Facts on File Inc, New York, 1961.

GANSHOF VAN DER MEERSCH, W. J.: *Fin de la souveraineté belge au Congo.* Martinus Nijhoff for Institut royal des relations internationales, The Hague, 1963.

GAVSHON, ARTHUR L.: *The Mysterious Death of Dag Hammarskjöld.* Walker, New York, 1962. (U.K. edition) *The Last Days of Dag Hammarskjöld.* Barrie & Rockliff with Pall Mall Press, London, 1963.

GERARD-LIBOIS, JULES: *Katanga Secession.* University of Wisconsin Press, Madison, 1966.

GILES, CHARLES-ANDRÉ: *Kasavubu: au coeur du drame congolaise.* Editions Europe-Afrique, Brussels, 1964.

GORDON, KING: *The United Nations in the Congo: A Quest for Peace.* Carnegie Endowment for International Peace, New York, 1962.

HEMPSTONE, SMITH: *Rebels, Mercenaries and Dividends: The Katanga Story.* Praeger, New York, 1962.

HOSKYNS, CATHERINE: *The Congo Since Independence: January 1960–December 1961.* Oxford University Press, 1965.

HOUART, PIERRE: *La Pénétration communist au Congo.* Centre de documentation internationale, Brussels, 1960.

HYMOFF, EDWARD: *Stig Von Bayer: International Troubleshooter for Peace.* James H. Heineman, New York, 1965.

JANSSENS, EMILE: *J'étais le général Janssens.* Charles Dessart, Brussels, 1961.

KANZA, THOMAS: *Congo 196–?.* Editions Remarques Congolaises, Brussels, 1962.

KITCHEN, HELEN (ed.): *Congo Story.* Walker & Co., New York, 1967.

LAWSON, RICHARD: *Strange Soldiering.* Hodder & Stoughton, London, 1963.

10

LECLERCQ, CLAUDE: *L'O.N.U. et l'Affaire du Congo*. Payot, Paris, 1964.

LEFEVER, ERNEST W.: *Uncertain Mandate—Policies of the U.N. Congo Operation*. Johns Hopkins Press, Baltimore, 1967.

LEFEVER, ERNEST W.: *Crisis in the Congo: a U.N. Force in Action*. Brookings Institution, Washington DC, 1965.

LEFEVER, ERNEST W. and WYNFRED, JOSHUA: *United Nations Peacekeeping in the Congo: 1960–1964—An Analysis of Political, Executive and Military Control*. Brookings Institution, Washington DC, 1966 (3 vols).

LEGUM, COLIN: *Congo Disaster*. Penguin Books, Baltimore, 1961.

LEMARCHAND, RENÉ: *Political Awakening in the Congo*. University of California Press, Berkeley, 1964.

LUMUMBA, PATRICE: *Congo My Country*. Pall Mall Press, London, 1962.

MERRIAN, ALAN P.: *Congo: Background of Conflict*. Northwestern University Press, Evanston, 1961.

MONHEIM, FRANCIS: *Mobutu, l'homme seul*. Editions Actuelles, Brussels, 1962.

O'BRIEN, CONOR CRUISE and TOPOLSKI, FELIKS: *United Nations: Sacred Drama*. Simon & Schuster, New York, 1968. Hutchinson, London, 1968.

O'BRIEN, CONOR CRUISE: *To Katanga and Back*. Simon & Schuster, New York, 1962.

OKUMU, WASHINGTON: *Lumumba's Congo: Roots of Conflict*. Obolensky, New York, 1963.

ROBERTS, JOHN: *My Congo Adventure*. Jarrold, London, 1963.

SCHUYLER, PHILIPPA: *Who Killed the Congo?* Devin Adair, New York, 1962.

SMITH, RAYMOND: *The Fighting Irish in the Congo*. Lilmac, Dublin, 1962.

TONDEL, LYMAN M., JR. (ed.): *The Legal Aspects of the United Nations Action in the Congo*. Oceana Publications, Dobbs Ferry, N.Y., 1963.

TRINQUIER, ROGER and OTHERS: *Notre Guerre au Katanga.* Editions de la pensée Moderne, Paris, 1963.

UNITED NATIONS: (Official U.N. 'White Book' on the Congo Operation) *The United Nations and the Congo: Some Salient Facts,* 1963.

VALAHU, MUGUR: *The Katanga Circus.* Robert Speller & Sons, New York, 1964.

VAN LANGENHOVE, FERNAND: *Le Role proéminent du Secretaire Général dans l'Operations des Nations Unies au Congo.* Institut Royal des Relations Internationales, Brussels, 1964.

WELENSKY, SIR ROY: Welensky's 400 Days. Collins, London, 1964.

YOUNG, CRAWFORD: *Politics in the Congo.* Princeton University Press, Princeton, 1965.

U.N. Peacekeeping—Cyprus Operation

BOYD, JAMES M.: *Cyprus: Episode in Peacekeeping.* Columbia University Press, 1966.

HARBOTTLE, Brigadier MICHAEL: *The Impartial Soldier.* Royal Institute of International Affairs, Oxford University Press, 1970.

HYMOFF, EDWARD: *Stig Von Bayer, International Trouble-shooter for Peace.* James H. Heineman, New York, 1965.

KYRIAKIDES, STANLEY: *Cyprus: Constitution and Crisis Government.* University of Pennsylvania, 1968.

MAYES, STANLEY: *Cyprus and Makarios.* Putnam, London, 1960.

SALIH, HALIL: *Cyprus: An Analysis of Cypriot Political Disorder.* Theo Gaus' Sons Inc., New York, 1968.

STEGENGA, JAMES: *The United Nations Force in Cyprus,* Columbia University Press, 1968.

STEPHENS, ROBERT: *Cyprus—A Place of Arms.* Pall Mall Press, London, 1966.

U.N. Peacekeeping—Asia Operations

HIGGINS, ROSALYN: *United Nations Peacekeeping: 1946–1967—Documents and Commentary. Vol. 2: Asia.* Oxford University Press, 1970.

TAYLOR, ALASTAIR: *Indonesia Independence and the United Nations.* London, 1960.

UNITED NATIONS: *The United Nations in West New Guinea.* New York, 1963.

ATTIA, G.: *Les forces armées des Nations Unies au Corée et au Moyen Orient.* Geneva, 1963.

BAILEY, S.: *The Korea Crisis.* London, 1950.

DAY, G.: *Le droit de veto dans l'organisation des Nations Unies.* Paris, 1952.

FRANKENSTEIN, MARC: *L'Organisation des Nations Unies devant le Conflit Coréen.* Pedone, Paris, 1952.

GOODRICH, LELAND M.: *Korea: A Study of U.S. Policy in the United Nations.* Harper Bros, New York, 1956.

LECKIE, ROBERT: *Conflict: The History of the Korean War 1950–53.* New York, 1962.

OSGOOD, ROBERT: *Limited War.* Chicago, 1957.

REES, DAVID: *Korea: The Limited War.* Macmillan, London, 1964.

AHMAD, MUSHAO: *The United Nations and Pakistan.* Pakistan Institute of International Affairs, Karachi, 1955.

Journals and Other Periodicals

Adelphi Papers: No. 9. Institute for Strategic Studies, London, 1964.

RIKHYE, I. J.: Preparation and Training of United Nations Peacekeeping Forces.

American Journal of International Law

HALDERMAN, JOHN W.: Legal Basis for United Nations Armed Forces. Vol. 56, No. 4; 1962; pp. 971–996.

MILLER, E. M.; Legal Aspects of the U.N. Action in the Congo. Vol. 55, No. 1; 1961; pp. 1–28.

NEIDLE, ALAN F.: Peacekeeping and Disarmament. Vol. 57, No. 1; 1963; pp. 46–72.

SOHN, LOUIS B.: The Authority of the United Nations to Establish and Maintain a Permanent United Nations Force. Vol. 52, No. 2; 1958; pp. 229 ff.

Archiv des Völkerrechts. Vol. 10, No. 3; 1963; pp. 257–272

LEYSER, JOHANNES: Dispute and Agreement on West New Guinea.

Australian Outlook

HEATHCOTE, NINA: American Policy Towards the U.N. Operation in the Congo. Vol. 18, No. 1; 1964; pp. 77–97.

MILLAR, T. B.: Kashmir, the Commonwealth, and the United Nations. Vol. 17, No. 1; 1963; pp. 54–73.

Australian Quarterly. June 1965

JASPAN, M. A.: West Irian: The First Two Years

British Institute of International and Comparative Law. London, 1960.

LAUTERPACHT, ELIHU: The U.N. Emergency Force: Basic Documents.

British Yearbook of International Law

SEYERSTED, FINN: United Nations Forces. Vol. 38; 1961; pp. 351–474.

SEYERSTED, FINN: United Nations Forces and the Laws of War. Vol. 39; 1962.

Canadian Army Journal. Vol. 17 (April 1963); pp. 110–120.

STETHEM, Col. H. W. C.: Signal Squadron in the Congo.

Conflict Resolution. Vol. VIII, No. 3; September 1964

WARREN, ROLAND: The Conflict Intersystem and the Change Agent.

Current Legal Problems. Vol. 12; London, 1959; pp. 247–268.

SCHWARZENBERG, G.: Problems of a United Nations Force.

Europa Archiv

HEINZE, CHRISTIAN: Der Zypern-konflikt, eine Bewährungs-probe Westlicher Friedensordnung. Vol. 19, No. 19; 1964; pp. 713–726.

KUNZMANN, KARL HEINZ: Aktuelle Vorschläge für eine Friedenstruppe der Vereinten Nationen. Vol. 13, 1958; pp. 10800–10826.

RIKHYE, INDAR JIT: Katanga als Schlüsselproblem für die Massnahmen der Vereinten Nationen im Kongo. Vol. 17, No. 18; 1962; pp. 610–627.

External Affairs (Ottawa)

MARTIN, PAUL: U.N. Peace-Keeping Operations in Cyprus. Vol. 16, No. 4; 1964; pp. 130–135.

MARTIN, PAUL: Role of the U.N. in Maintaining Peace and Security. Vol. 16, No. 4; 1964; pp. 149–154.

MARTIN, PAUL: Some Improvisations in United Nations Peace-Keeping. Vol. 16, No. 8; 1964; pp. 373–377.

Foreign Affairs

ARMSTRONG, HAMILTON FISH: The United Nations Experience in Gaza. Vol. 35, No. 4; 1957; pp. 600–619.

ARMSTRONG, HAMILTON FISH: U.N. on Trial. Vol. 39, No. 3; 1961; pp. 388–415.

DOUGLAS, PAUL H.: United To Enforce Peace. Vol. 30, No. 1; 1951; pp. 1–16.

HAEKKERUP, PER: Scandinavia's Peace-Keeping Forces for the U.N. Vol. 41, No. 2; 1964; pp. 675–681.

MUNRO, SIR LESLIE: Can the United Nations Enforce Peace? Vol. 38, No. 2; 1960; pp. 209–218.

PEARSON, LESTER B.: Force for the U.N. Vol. 35, No. 3; 1957; pp. 395–404.

Harpers. Vol. 221; November 1960; pp. 75–84

KRAFT, JOSEPH: The Untold Story of the U.N.'s Congo Army.

India Quarterly
BARSTON, RONALD P.: Greek–Turkish Cypriot Relations and the Cyprus Problem. March 1971.
International Affairs (London)
MARTIN, PAUL: Peace-Keeping and the United Nations—The Broader View. Vol. 40, No. 2; 1964; pp. 191–204.
O'DONOVAN, PATRICK: The precedent of the Congo. Vol. 37, No. 2; 1961; pp. 181–188.
SPRY, GRAHAM: Canada, the United Nations Emergency Force and the Commonwealth. Vol. 33, No. 3; 1957; pp. 289–300.
VAN BILSON, A. A. J.: Some Aspects of the Congo Problem. Vol. 38; January 1962; pp. 41–52.
WIGNY, PIERRE: Belgium and the Congo. Vol. 37; July 1961.
International and Comparative Law Quarterly. Vol. 12; April 1963; pp. 387–413
DRAPER, G. I. A. D.: The Legal Limitations upon the Employment of Weapons by the United Nations Force in the Congo.
International Conciliation
CLAUDE, INIS L., JR.: The United Nations and the Use of Force. No. 532; March 1961; pp. 325–384.
COLLINS, J. FOSTER: The United Nations and Indonesia. No. 459; 1950; pp. 115–200.
GOODRICH, LELAND M.: Korea: Collective Measures against Aggression. No. 494; 1953; pp. 129–192.
LEONARD, L. LARRY: The United Nations and Palestine. No. 454; 1949; pp. 607–786.
MOHN, PAUL: Problems of Truce Supervision. No. 478; 1952; pp. 51–99
International Journal (Toronto)
BISHOP, PETER V.: UNOPAX: A New Name (with a definition) for U.N. Peace-Keeping Operations. Vol. 18, No. 4; 1963; pp. 525–531.

COHEN, MAXWELL: The United Nations Emergency Force: A Preliminary View. Vol. 12, No. 2; 1957; pp. 109–127.

GORDON, KING: The U.N. in Cyprus. Vol. 19, No. 3; 1964; pp. 326–347.

HOLMES, JOHN: The U.N. in the Congo. Vol. 16, No. 1; 1961; pp. 1–16.

KOTANI, HIDEJIRO: Peace-Keeping Problems for Smaller Countries. Vol. 19, No. 3; 1964; pp. 308–325.

MURRAY, G. S.: United Nations Peacekeeping and Problems of International Control. Vol. 18, No. 4; 1963; pp. 442–457.

International Organization

BLOOMFIELD, Lincoln P.: Headquarters—Field Relations: Some Notes on the Beginning and End of ONUC. Vol. 17, No. 2; 1963; pp. 377–392.

BLOOMFIELD, LINCOLN P.: Peacekeeping in a Disarming —but Revolutionary—World. Vol. 17, No. 2; 1963; pp. 444–464.

BOWMAN, E. H. and FANNING, J. E.: The Logistic Problems of a U.N. Military Force. Vol. 17, No. 2; 1963; pp. 355–376.

DICKS, HENRY V.: National Loyalty, Identity and the International Soldier. Vol. 17, No. 2; 1963; pp. 425–443.

GOODRICH, LELAND M. and ROSNER, GABRIELLA E.: The United Nations Emergency Force. Vol. 11; 1957; pp. 413–430.

GROSS, LEO: Expenses of the United Nations for Peace-Keeping Operations: The Advisory Opinion of the International Court of Justice. Vol. 17, No. 1; 1963; pp. 1–35.

HOFFMAN, STANLEY: In Search of a Thread: The UN in the Congo Labyrinth. Vol. 16, No. 2; 1962; pp. 331–361.

HOFFMAN, STANLEY: Sisyphus and the Avalanche: The United Nations, Egypt and Hungary. Vol. 11; 1957; pp. 446–469.

HOFFMAN, STANLEY: Erewhon or Lilliput?—a Critical View of the Idea of Internationalized Force. Vol. 17, No. 2; 1963; pp. 404–424.

HUREVITZ, J. C.: The United Nations Conciliation Commission for Palestine. Vol. 7; 1953; pp. 482–497.

KORBEL, JOSEF: The Kashmir Dispute and the United Nations. Vol. 3, No. 2; 1949; pp. 278–287.

KORBEL, JOSEF: The Kashmir Dispute After Six Years. Vol. 7, No. 4; 1953; pp. 498–510.

LOURIE, SYLVIA: The United Nations Military Observer Group in India and Pakistan. Vol. 9, No. 1; 1955; pp. 19–31.

MORGENTHAU, HANS J.: The Political Conditions for an International Force. Vol. 17, No.2; 1963; pp. 393–403.

NICHOLAS, HERBERT: U.N. Peace Forces and the Changing Globe: The Lessons of Suez and Congo. Vol. 17, No. 2; 1963; pp. 321–337.

PERKINS, WHITNEY T.: Sanctions for Political Change—The Indonesian Case. Vol. 12, No. 1; 1958; pp. 26–42.

PETERSEN, KEITH S.: The Uses of the Uniting for Peace Resolution Since 1950. Vol. 13, No. 2; 1959; pp. 219–232.

SCHELLING, THOMAS C.: Strategic Problems of An International Force in a Disarmed World. Vol. 17, No. 2; 1963; pp. 465–485.

URQUHART, BRIAN: United Nations Peace Forces and the Changing United Nations—An Institutional Perspective. Vol. 17, No. 2; 1963; pp. 338–354.

VAN DER VEUR, PAUL W.: The U.N. and West Irian: A Critique. Vol. 18, No. 1; 1964; pp. 53–73.

WEST, R. L.: The United Nations and the Congo Financial Crisis: Lessons of the First Year. Vol. 15, No. 3; 1961; pp. 603–617.

Internasjonal Politikk. No. 3; 1961; pp. 250–265
STOKKE, OLAV: United Nations Emergency Force—et Politisk instrument.

International Relations

BARSTON, RONALD P.: Problems in International Peace-keeping: the Case for Cyprus. March 1971.

BENTWICH, NORMAN: Israel–Syrian Armistice Agreement (1967).

KAY, ZACHARIAH: The U.N. in Korea and Sinai. Vol. 2, No.3; 1961; pp. 168–183.

International Studies Association Proceedings. April 1965; pp. 49–63

GULLION, EDMUND: Crisis Management: Lessons from the Congo (Crises and Concepts in International Affairs).

International Studies (New Delhi). Vol. 4, No. 4; 1963

AGWAMI, M. S.: The Lebanese Crisis in Retrospect.

Journal of Conflict Resolution. Vol. 7, No. 2; 1963; pp. 117–129

CLAUDE, INIS L.: United Nations Use of Military Force.

Journal of Contemporary History. July 1968

HIGGINS, ROSALYN: The June War: United Nations and Legal Background.

Keesing's Contemporary Archives. 1948–1971

Macleans. May 2, 1964

PEARSON, LESTER B.: A New Kind of Peace Force.

Norsk Militaert Tidsskrift

BULL, ODD: De Forente Nasjoners Observatørgruppe i Lebanon i 1958. Vol. 129, Nos. 8–9; 1959; pp. 543–570, 618–642.

DALE, TORSTEIN: Sikkerhetsstyrker for FN. Vol. 134, No. 8; 1964; pp. 540–551.

Orbis. Vol. 7, No. 1; 1963; pp. 120–149

VAN DER KROEF, JUSTUS M.: The West New Guinea Settlement: Its Origins and Implications.

Osterreichische Zeitschrift für Öffentliches Recht. Vol. 12; 1962; pp. 188–229

SEYERSTED, FINN: Can the United Nations Establish Military Forces and Perform Other Acts Without Specific Basis in the Charter?

Politique Etrangère. Vol. 20, No. 2; 1955
GIRAUD, EMILE: Les Nations Unies doivent-elles mettre en veilleuse la sécurité collective?
Survival. Vol. 6, No. 4; 1964; pp. 150–158
PEARSON, LESTER B.: Keeping the Peace.
The New Leader. November 7, 1960
DRAPER, THEODORE: Ordeal of the U.N.: Kruschev, Hammarskjöld, and the Congo Crisis.
The University of Chicago Law Review. Vol. 33, No. 2; 1966; pp. 249–315
NATHANSON, NATHANIEL L.: Constitutional Crisis at the United Nations: The Price of Peacekeeping.
The World Today. Journal of the Royal Institute of International Affairs, London
HIGGINS, ROSALYN: Basic Facts on the U.N. Force in Cyprus, Vol. 20, No. 8; 1964; pp. 347–350
JAMES, ALAN: U.N. Action for Peace: I.—Barrier Forces; Vol. 18, No. 11; 1962; pp. 478–486. II.—Law and Order Forces; Vol. 18, No. 12; 1962; pp. 504–513
The Yale Review. Vol. 43; 1954; pp. 481–496
WOLFERS, ARNOLD: Collective Security and the War in Korea.
World Politics. XVII (October 1964); pp. 75–107
JACOBSON, HAROLD K.—ONUC'S Civilian Operations: State-Preserving and State-Building.
Zeitschrift für Ausländisches Offentliches Recht und Völkerrecht. Vol. 19; 1959; pp. 389–415
SCHEUNER, ULRICH: Eine Internationale Sicherungsmacht im Dienste der Vereinten Nationen.

ADDENDUM

The Military Law and Law War Review. G. I. A. D. DRAPER.
UN Forces (including UNEF). Vol. V, No. 1; 1966; pp. 45–61.
UN Force in Congo (ONUC). Vol. V, No. 2; 1966; pp. 377–405.
UN Force in Cyprus (UNFICYP). Vol. VI, No. 1; 1967; pp. 51–75.

APPENDIX 1

MAJOR UNITED NATIONS PEACEKEEPING OPERATIONS

	UNEF (UN Emergency Force)	UNOGIL (UN Observer Group in Lebanon)	ONUC (UN Congo Operation)	UNSF (UN Security Force)	UNYOM (UN Yemen Observation Group)
Location	Egypt–Israel border	Lebanon	Congo	West Irian	Yemen
Duration	1956–1967 (10 yrs 6 mos)	1958 (6 mos)	1960–1964 (4 yrs)	1962–1963 (9 mos)	1963–1964 (1 yr 3 mos)
Type of crisis	inter-state	internal with external involvement	internal	inter-state	internal with external involvement
Function of the Force	border patrol	border patrol	internal pacification	internal pacification	internal pacification
Establishment	General Assembly	Security Council	Security Council	General Assembly	Security Council
Size	max. 6,000	600	max 20,000	1,600	200
Estimated Cost	$220,000,000	$4,000,000	$450,000,000	$6,000,000	$3,000,000
Countries providing contingents of military or police personnel	Canada Yugoslavia India Indonesia Brazil Colombia Denmark Sweden Norway Finland	Italy Denmark Norway Canada Netherlands India Sweden Finland (+ small contingents from 13 other countries)	India, Morocco, Tunisia, Ethiopia, Ghana, Nigeria, Malaya, Ireland, Indonesia, Sweden, Guinea, Mali, Pakistan, UAR, Sudan, Liberia (+ small contingents from 19 other countries)	Pakistan United States Canada Brazil Ceylon India Ireland Nigeria Sweden	Yugoslavia Canada Denmark India Itay Netherlands Norway Ghana Pakistan Sweden
Countries providing the bulk of the financial support (with approximate % of the total cost of the peacekeeping operation	USA (48%) UK (12) France (9) Canada (4) India (3) Italy (3) Japan (2) Australia (2)	USA (33%) USSR (14) UK (8) France (6) China (5) Canada (3) India (2) Italy (2)	USA (48%) UK (10) Canada (4) Italy (3) India (2) Japan (2) Sweden (2) Netherlands (2)	Netherlands (50%) Indonesia (50)	Saudi Arabia (50%) UAR (50)

UNFICYP (UN Force in Cyprus)	UNTSO (UN Truce Supervisory Mission)	UNMOGIP (UN Military Observer Group India/Pakistan)	UNIPOM (UN India and Pakistan Observer Mission)	UN Force in Korea
Cyprus	Palestine/Israel	Kashmir	India–Pakistan border	North/South Korea
1964–1971 (7 yrs)	1948–1971 (23 yrs +)	1949–1971 (22 yrs +)	1965–1966 (6 mos)	1950–1953 (3 yrs 1 mo)
internal with external involvement	inter-state	inter-state	inter-state	inter-state
internal pacification	observation of armistice lines	observation of armistice line	border patrol	enforcement action
Security Council	Security Council	Security Council	Security Council	Security Council
max 6,500	max 500	max 89	82 (93)*	740,000
$170,000,000	$25–30,000,000	$10–15,000,000	$2,000,000	see below
UK Canada Sweden Denmark Finland Austria Australia New Zealand Ireland	Australia Belgium Canada Denmark Finland France Ireland Italy Netherlands New Zealand Norway Sweden USA Austria Argentina Burma Chile	Australia Belgium Canada Chile Denmark Finland Italy Mexico New Zealand Norway Sweden Uruguay USA	Brazil Burma Canada Ceylon Ethiopia Ireland Nepal Netherlands Nigeria Venezuela	Australia Belgium, Canada, Colombia, Cuba, Denmark, Ethiopia, France, Greece, India, Italy, Luxembourg, Netherlands, New Zealand, Norway Philippines, S. Africa, S. Korea, Sweden, Thailand, Turkey, UK, USA
USA (35%) UK (27) Canada (12) W.Germany (5) Greece (5) Italy (1) Sweden (1) Turkey (1)	Financed out of regular UN budget as a Special Mission and is paid for from UN members' annual contributions	Financed out of regular UN budget as a Special Mission and is paid for from UN members' annual contributions	Financed out of regular UN budget as a Special Mission and is paid for from UN members' annual contributions	Fiscal agreements arranged between Republic of Korea and contributing governments

* Unofficial maximum figure.

INDEX